# *Routledge Revivals*

# Envoy Extraordinary

First published in 1965, *Envoy Extraordinary* is a detailed biographical study of Vijaya Lakshmi Pandit and her contribution to India.

Drawing on a wealth of interviews, press-cuttings, speeches, letters, and more, the book delves into Vijaya Lakshmi Pandit's political and diplomatic career and explores her personal values and ideals. It adopts an objective and truthful approach that does not steer away from the more difficult or disconcerting aspects of Pandit's private and public life. In doing so, it provides a thorough study of her career and a detailed insight into India's political history.

# Envoy Extraordinary

A Study of Vijaya Lakshmi Pandit and Her Contribution to Modern India

By Vera Brittain

First published in 1965
by George Allen & Unwin Ltd.

This edition first published in 2021 by Routledge
2 Park Square, Milton Park, Abingdon, Oxon, OX14 4RN
and by Routledge
605 Third Avenue, New York, NY 10017

*Routledge is an imprint of the Taylor & Francis Group, an informa business*

© Vera Brittain, 1965

All rights reserved. No part of this book may be reprinted or reproduced or utilised in any form or by any electronic, mechanical, or other means, now known or hereafter invented, including photocopying and recording, or in any information storage or retrieval system, without permission in writing from the publishers.

**Publisher's Note**
The publisher has gone to great lengths to ensure the quality of this reprint but points out that some imperfections in the original copies may be apparent.

**Disclaimer**
The publisher has made every effort to trace copyright holders and welcomes correspondence from those they have been unable to contact.

A Library of Congress record exists under LCCN: 65089998

ISBN 13: 978-0-367-69012-0 (hbk)
ISBN 13: 978-1-003-14003-0 (ebk)

# Envoy
# Extraordinary

A STUDY OF VIJAYA LAKSHMI PANDIT
AND HER CONTRIBUTION TO MODERN INDIA

BY VERA BRITTAIN

*London*
GEORGE ALLEN & UNWIN LTD
RUSKIN HOUSE MUSEUM STREET

FIRST PUBLISHED IN 1965

*This book is copyright under the Berne Convention. Apart from any fair dealing for the purposes of private study, research, criticism or review, as permitted under the Copyright Act, 1956, no portion may be reproduced by any process without written permission. Enquiries should be addressed to the publishers.*

© *George Allen & Unwin Ltd., 1965*

# CONTENTS

| | | |
|---|---|---|
| FOREWORD | *The Pacemaker* | 11 |
| 1. | *An Indian Prison* | 21 |
| 2. | *A Prisoner Remembers* | 31 |
| 3. | *Family in Revolt* | 43 |
| 4. | *The Cost of a Crusade* | 52 |
| 5. | *Courage in Herself* | 62 |
| 6. | *Crusader into Ambassador* | 74 |
| 7. | *Soviet Citadel* | 83 |
| 8. | *Washington Embassy* | 95 |
| 9. | *United Nations* | 108 |
| 10. | *The Conquest of Britain* | 122 |
| 11. | *Bombay and After* | 141 |
| 12. | *Nightfall on the Jumna* | 159 |
| EPILOGUE | *The Torch-Bearer* | 166 |
| APPENDIX | | 169 |
| INDEX | | 171 |

# ACKNOWLEDGEMENTS

My first debt of gratitude is due to Mrs Pandit herself, for allowing me to write about her; for finding time in her crowded life for long interviews; for the loan of books, press-cuttings and speeches; for permission to quote letters; and for most generous private hospitality on two occasions in Bombay. No 'subject' of a biography could have been more helpful and co-operative. But I am also deeply indebted to the late Prime Minister of India, Mr Jawaharlal Nehru, for authorizing this book, and by his friendly comments encouraging me to write it; and to Mrs Pandit's daughters, Chandalekra, Nayantara, and Rita, for their kindly support and several useful discussions.

Much gratitude is also due to the Hon Hamayun Kabir, then Minister of Scientific Research and Cultural Affairs, who sponsored my tour of India in January and February 1963.

I am most grateful to HE the Deputy High Commissioner for India, Mr Kewal Singh, for helpful advice especially with regard to Indian officials in Washington; to Mr U. S. Bajpai, Consular Political Officer, for assistance with the use of publications at India House, London; to the officials at India House, and especially Mr Rajendranath Gupta, Public Relations Officer, and Mr N. N. Gupta, Information Attaché, for the loan of many newspapers and magazines, and for their consistent helpfulness; and to Mr Sunder Kabadi, Head of the Indian Press in London, for the gift of press-cuttings and much useful information.

I am greatly indebted to the Indian Embassy officials in Washington, and especially to the Chief Information Officer, Mr J. N. Ganju, and to several distinguished American State Department officials who prefer to remain anonymous.

I also wish to thank most gratefully the Hon. Adlai Stevenson and his Secretaries, Miss Davidoff and Miss Edenein, for help and information at the United Nations Headquarters in New York; Mrs Ruth Gage Colby, of the UN Press Department, for data and information about Mrs Pandit's work at the United Nations on various dates; and the

# 10                  *Envoy Extraordinary*

Library officials at the UN Information Centre, Stratford Place, London, for their willing assistance.

I am indebted to the Fawcett Library, Wilfred Street, Westminster, for the use of books and press-cuttings; to Mr Richard Bright, Television Publicity Officer, for the transcripts of an interview between Mrs Pandit and Mr Ludovic Kennedy, broadcast in July 1961, and of a programme featuring the life of Mr Nehru broadcast in February 1962; to Miss Christina Foyle for the transcript of a speech by Mrs Pandit at a Foyle's Luncheon in 1961; to Begum Shaista Ikramullah of Pakistan and Mr S. A. Hasan for valuable information; to Mrs Noreen Parkes, personal Secretary to the Indian High Commissioners in London, for consistent practical help and advice; and to the Central Office of Information and the Oxford *Mail and Times* for their help in connection with Mrs Pandit's Oxford visit in October 1964.

It is difficult adequately to express my gratitude to Miss Irene Harrison, one of Mrs Pandit's best friends in London, for reading the manuscript and offering me her constructive criticisms; and to my husband Professor George Catlin, both for performing a similar service, and for valuable introductions in the United States, especially at the State Department in Washington.

Very special thanks are also due to Mr Edward Halliday, who painted the portrait of Mrs Pandit which hangs in India House, London, and to HE Dr Jivraj Mehta, the High Commissioner, for their kind permission to use it as the frontispiece of this book.

Finally, I would like to record my indebtedness to the remarkable group of journalists who attended Mr Nehru's funeral in May 1964, and particularly to the Special Correspondent of *The Times*; Tom Stacey of the *Sunday Times* and its special photographers Marc Riboud and Marilyn Silverstone; Anne Sharpley of the *Evening Standard*; and Vincent Mulchrone and Simon Roy of the *Daily Mail*.

If I have inadvertently omitted anyone who has kindly helped me with advice and information for a book which has required nearly four years of intermittent research and travel in three countries (Britain, India and the United States), I can only offer my apologies and express my gratitude.

VERA BRITTAIN.

*December 1964.*

FOREWORD

# The Pacemaker

WHEN Jawaharlal[1] Nehru died on May 27, 1964, an era in which the history of modern India and the story of the Nehru dynasty were virtually synonymous ended in tragic majesty. Henceforward members of the family and not least his sister Vijaya Lakshmi Pandit, eleven years his junior and unrivalled in her experience of foreign affairs, will continue to play their part, but it is unlikely to be the same part, and it cannot be in the same India.

After this overwhelming twentieth century has been assessed by those who come after us, the conclusion may well be reached that no one of its titanic figures—not Lenin, nor Mahatma Gandhi, nor Winston Churchill—made a more impressive personal contribution to the history of our apocalyptic era than Prime Minister Nehru. Whatever the personal failures and shortcomings which he was always the first to acknowledge, his work shaped the future not only of India but of Asia, and by opening the door of the Commonwealth to non-white races, made it the multi-racial symbol of human equality into which it has grown during the past two decades. Today an instrument of world unity has replaced the power-pursuing colonial empire of the two previous centuries.

This seems therefore a timely moment for trying to estimate and interpret Mrs Pandit's important part in the making of modern India from the time that Gandhi returned from South Africa when she was still a child, and brought the entire Nehru household into the movement for independence. She bore her full share of the pains, penalties and sacrifices arising from this movement, and later assumed a larger rôle in creating the diplomacy of the new India than any outstanding Indian apart from Mr Nehru himself. This part has in fact been unique in the history of diplomacy as such. No other diplomat, man or woman, has carried within a period of fifteen years the Ambassadorship to three major powers and the Presidency of the United Nations.

[1]The name means 'Red Jewel'.

## 12       *Envoy Extraordinary*

I first had the idea of writing this book some four years ago, and of including in it much more about her diplomatic achievements against their international background than other studies of her work and personality either in books or in articles. Mr Nehru, whom I had met periodically through the years since he was our guest in Chelsea during a brief period out of prison in 1936, himself responded favourably to the suggestion, and from Mrs Pandit I have had the maximum co-operation possible to her amid a public programme of fantastic dimensions. In fact it was not until she was free from the heavy burden of work arising from her post as High Commissioner in London from 1954 to 1961, and my husband and I went to India as guests of its Government early in 1963, that I was able to make much progress.

At that time we stayed with her for several days at Raj Bhawan, the Governor's House in Bombay. She then gave me the opportunity of 'interviewing' her on various occasions, and lent me numerous articles and press-cuttings, and the services of the excellent secretary who copied them for me. I shall long remember two evenings in which we sat on her balcony and talked of the more personal aspects of her life while the sun set in copper-hued splendour over the Arabian Sea.

A subsequent visit to Washington and much assistance from friendly officials at India House in London, in addition to gifts by the Cultural Ministry in Delhi of relevant books and pamphlets, enabled me to see the diplomatic background in clearer perspective.

When I was in India gathering material, a distinguished Indian woman who had known the subject of my book all her life firmly expressed her doubt whether an Englishwoman could sufficiently understand an Indian to write her biography. She also questioned whether my personal knowledge of Mrs Pandit was equal to the task.

These were reasonable doubts which may well prove to be justified, but I want nevertheless to attempt an answer to them. I will deal with the second objection first.

In my own experience there are three main types of biography. The first, as in all historical biographies, is that in which the writer does not know the subject at all, and has to kindle life from the often very dry bones of contemporary documents. I attempted this kind in an un-ambitious study of John Bunyan, produced for Rich and Cowan's *In the Steps* series in 1950. From this work I learned that a dead subject can indeed live again in terms of contemporary or near-contemporary impressions, but most of all from his own words in so far as these are recorded in books, letters and speeches.

The opposite type of biography is that in which the writer knows the

# The Pacemaker

subject intimately, and is emotionally involved. Leaving aside the special category of autobiography—where emotional involvement is at maximum but the writer knows the subject only up to a point because the problem of seeing himself as others see him can never be completely mastered and he has to steer between the Scylla of self-flattery and the equally formidable Charybdis of excessive diffidence—I attempted the intimate biography in *Testament of Friendship*, the story of Winifred Holtby, the incomparable friend of my youth. Though I struggled for detachment I was not, I think, successful; I had been too close to her to achieve it, and was throughout too sorrowfully possessed by the tragedy of the untimely illness (today probably curable) that cut off the vivid magnanimous life with which she would have done so much.

Again leaving aside the 'debunkers' with their ephemeral malice, there remains a third biographical category in which the writer knows, likes and respects the subject, but not to that degree of intimacy which makes detachment unattainable. I attempted this in my 'Portrait' of Lord Pethick-Lawrence, a valued but not an intimate friend, on whose account I had to project myself into another generation and the opposite sex. In contemplating Mrs Pandit I am handicapped by neither biological nor chronological differences, for we belong to the same sex and are approximately contemporaries.

The first objection—the fact that she belongs to a different race and nationality from myself—does of course remain, and I am well aware that in her are racial depths to which I shall never penetrate. But I am inclined, and I hope not too optimistically, to believe that the shrinkage of the world and the development of psychological insight —both phenomena of the twentieth century—have minimized the significance of such distinctions. Today differences of experience and of values, which can occur as much within as between races, create higher barriers than differences of colour, nationality, and even background. When modern travel makes relatively frequent meetings possible between the citizens of different countries, and letters and conversations can be shared between them with full understanding, the arbitrary obstacles once created by national and racial contrasts tend to diminish.

For me Vijaya Lakshmi Pandit is not so much a woman or an Indian as a pacemaker—a symbolic example for all countries and both sexes. She has been especially a pacemaker for women because the development rate of women everywhere so urgently needs to be galvanized, but she is also a pacemaker for diplomats of both sexes because she has brought into diplomacy a special quality due not to 'intuition' but to

# 14 *Envoy Extraordinary*

the sensitive comprehension of human problems which women derive from their personal and family experience.

Now that men, particularly of the younger generations, are so widely acquiring the arts of fatherhood, and becoming proficient in the minor domestic skills of which a mastery has been made necessary for all citizens by the growth of democracy and the gradual elimination of household wage-slaves, women may not much longer have a virtual monopoly of such knowledge. But at present they possess it and, when they obtain the opportunity, can modify the over-rigid traditions of the diplomatic and political world in the direction of greater humanity. In this direction lies one answer to the problem of war. Here too a woman diplomat can be a pacemaker, particularly when, like Mrs Pandit, she has a closer acquaintance than most male diplomats with the councils of international assemblies and the ethics of treaty-making, and was trained during her youth in the unique school of philosophic and practical non-violence created by Mahatma Gandhi.

Apart from a knowledge of many countries, a love of travel, and a capacity for adaptation to new circumstances which with her amounts to genius, I have shared with Mrs Pandit two formative emotional experiences: the official and frustrating dislike of the rebel by the wielders of power, and the bitter need arising from the cruelties of a political environment to part with young children at a crucial stage in their development. Both these experiences belonged to the Second World War, but their consequences though not their bitterness live on.

At the very time (1940–45) when Vijaya Lakshmi Pandit was a stormy and effective rebel against the Indian policy of the British Government, I too was a rebel against its war-time policies—not to its actual opposition to the dictators, but to such methods of war-making as blockade, which especially penalized the mothers and children of Occupied Europe, and obliteration bombing, which led straight to nuclear warfare and the tentative quality of man's present life on earth. I was also, with my husband, a keen and vocal advocate of Indian independence at a time when the war-waging British Government wanted as little as possible said in public about blockade, massacre bombing, and the claims of India.

These dual forms of rebellion made it impossible for Mrs Pandit and myself, who then knew each other only by name, to develop a closer acquaintance during the war. She spent much of it in prison, as my first three chapters describe, and though I was never imprisoned, I was often close to that politer form of incarceration known as 'detention'. One form of detention I actually did suffer; between 1940 and 1945 I

# The Pacemaker

was not permitted to leave Britain and exercise my rebellious voice in other countries. This meant that when Mrs Pandit, as President of the All-India Women's Conference in 1940-41, invited me to attend its 1941 annual meeting as a British delegate, I was obliged to decline. I could not, I found, obtain permission to go, though thanks to the good offices of Agatha Harrison and Mrs Corbett Ashby, I got as far as a humiliating interview with Mr Leo Amery, then Secretary of State for India.

During this same period Mrs Pandit and her husband (who died in 1944 from the consequences of imprisonment) sent their two elder daughters to be educated in the United States, since neither in India nor in Britain could the student activities of courageous young women be guaranteed to keep them out of prison. Early in the war my own son and daughter, then small children younger than hers, also went to America to be rescued, not from bombs, but from the possible consequences for the offspring of political rebels when invasion threatened in 1940. Five years later, when my husband and I found ourselves on the Gestapo list of those who would have been shot or imprisoned had the Nazis landed, and I learned that I was equally obnoxious to Hitler's minions and the British Home Office, we realized that our much criticized decision had, like hers, been right.

I suspect that the shared sorrow and anxiety of parting with our children at a time of maximum international danger means far more to Mrs Pandit and myself than the accident that she was born in Allahabad and I in Newcastle-under-Lyme. But some differences in our Eastern and Western backgrounds must be understood, and these relate not least to the position of women.

In India there have been vast actual inequalities between men and women due to religious and social practice, and a far higher rate of illiteracy among women which created a barrier between themselves and the world of knowledge. But no *theory* of inequality existed. 'It has simply been taken for granted that men and women are equal,' Mrs Pandit wrote in a *Punch* article, 'The Second Sex', published on May 16, 1962, 'and even though some centuries separated the period when woman functioned as a free citizen in her own right and her re-emergence after India's independence, the theoretical acceptance of equality has always remained'.

The Vedas, she continued, taught that women should be given equal opportunities with men in education and social activities, and the building-up of Indian culture included the work of women philosophers, scholars, poets, queens and administrators: 'they functioned

# 16                    *Envoy Extraordinary*

freely as individuals and rose to heights of greatness and achievement.' But the ancient law-givers, such as Manu, changed this pattern, and deprived women of their high status by laws which made them dependent on men. Muslim rule in India, by still further denying opportunities to women, increased the deterioration of Hindu society. It continued in the North till the middle of the eighteenth century: all the area was under Muslim influence, but purdah was never practised in the West and South. Though the British introduced a measure of female education, they also carried to India the contemporary Western notions of woman's 'place'.

In Western Europe a good deal of practical equality had existed—especially perhaps in France, where acquiescent men tended to marry strong and dominant women—but the practice of social equality was combined with an inelastic theory of female inferiority and subservience. Throughout the nineteenth century this theory found expression in unequal pay in industry and the professions, the non-appointment of qualified women to important posts in business and the Civil and Diplomatic Services, and even after the suffrage movement began, by the published views of politicians, medical theorists such as Sir Almroth Wright, and amateur male sociologists who were strangely reinforced by a few eminent detractors of their own sex, such as Gertrude Bell and Mrs Humphry Ward.

Since, as Virginia Woolf has written, ideas are 'tough as roots and intangible as sea-mist', and thus much harder to fight than legal and economic regulations, there had to be a suffrage movement in Britain to change the thought-habits of the normal English man and woman. This movement was middle-class because at that time only middle-class women were sufficiently educated to produce the necessary evidence to demolish the long-accepted theories.

In India a suffrage movement was unnecessary because no ineluctable theory had to be changed: it proved essential only to provide women with the actual practice of power all the way from the picketing of shops to Ministerial authority. This exercise of initiative, which in itself destroyed taboos, Mahatma Gandhi furnished by calling women out of their homes to take part in the Independence movement, and by giving them in his writings sufficient sustaining theory to remove any doubts which the more conservative might entertain.

'I am firmly of opinion,' he said, 'that India's salvation depends on the sacrifices and enlightenment of her women'. His call was not to middle-class women but to all women who cared for their country's independence, from the well-to-do subordinated wives of public men

# The Pacemaker 17

to peasant women working in the fields. Even today there are women in India's Parliament who are hardly literate, but who bring to their work a sound practical knowledge of village administration.

Thus emancipation has come in India without sex antagonism, the psychological trouble-maker which still tends to bedevil both professional and matrimonial relations in the West, and particularly in Europe. A number of highly educated Indian women were sufficiently influenced by the British suffrage movement to establish in the nineteen-twenties the All-India Women's Conference which demanded social and educational reform, but its foundation came after Gandhi had given them all a new conception of women's function in the world.

A few pacemakers were none the less necessary to show what democratic women could achieve, and Mrs Pandit, who consistently acknowledges her debt to the great poet and administrator, Sarojini Naidu, had been one of the foremost of these in a field where until very recently the appointment of a woman as Third Secretary to a diplomatic mission was regarded by Western governments as a dangerous innovation.

According to an article in the Bombay *Onlooker*, written when Mrs Pandit was India's High Commissioner in London, she feels that amid her many honours and triumphs, 'the greatest satisfaction of all has been the thought that, in however small a way, one was helping to dispel the age-old tradition that woman could not do man's work'.

Other Indian women pioneers have included the late Rajkumari Amrit Kaur, once Gandhi's Secretary and more recently Minister of Health; Mrs Hansa Mehta, a former Vice-Chancellor of the University of Baroda; Mrs Lakshmi Menon, Minister of State; and Miss Padmaja Naidu, Mrs Naidu's daughter who is now Governor of West Bengal. But Mrs Pandit has held more key positions than any woman up to date, and certainly more than most men. There have been other women Ambassadors, but never one who has represented her country in all the world's dominant centres of power.

With Motilal Nehru as her father and Jawaharlal as her brother her inheritance could have been a heavy burden, of which she might have made much or relatively little. But she was never overwhelmed by this heritage, though added to it were gifts, carrying responsibilities as well as advantages, such as the traditional fairy godmother confers on the specially favoured female infant. These gifts included spontaneous charm and grace, a delicate petite beauty, and a keen natural intelligence, now highly polished by experience, which provides an element

B

# 18 *Envoy Extraordinary*

of piquant incongruity when it is vigorously levied against her opponents in international debate. Part of the force which came from its unexpectedness is now mitigated since it is unexpected no longer, but this loss is more than compensated by the authority which her personal history conveys.

If she has not been carried away by success and adulation, the reason is almost certainly that, like nearly all who possess some quality of greatness, she has known enough adversity to counterbalance the good fortune. The sudden transformation of a secure and luxurious home into a volcanic centre of experimental hazards for political purposes; the cruel frustration of youthful passion by the same all-devouring national ends; prolonged periods of imprisonment; the early death of a husband who had proved to be an ideal companion; the experience of parting with two young daughters amid the risks and anxieties of the war; the loss of beloved and irreplaceable friends at times of maximum responsibility; and until recently the self-discipline imposed, often painfully, by the stern determination of her famous brother to permit no personal concessions which might justify charges of nepotism—all these things have tempered her amiable and generous qualities to the hardness and sharpness of steel. Jawaharlal's death finally provided a crown of sorrow which brought to her, as to India, a greater challenge than any she had yet confronted.

Her sterner qualities, ruthlessly moulded by the bitterness of experience, determined my own choices when I had to decide what kind of book to write. A distinguished and beautiful woman can be—and in various publications has been—presented to the reader in a eulogistic and agreeable *pastiche*, of the type favoured by Women's Clubs and glossy magazines, which emphasizes the personal and often the more trivial aspects of the subject while playing down the weightier political and diplomatic background. But hagiolatry of this type has never been my métier, which has led me to attempt objective studies consistent with my reading of history and my understanding of facts in so far as I know them.

Perhaps the most difficult problem has arisen from the friendly hospitality received so long and so often from the Indian Government, both at home and abroad, and from the great generosity shown to me by Mrs Pandit herself and her family as soon as I was permitted the privilege of writing her story. How far would the facts, if they proved to be uncomfortable and even at times unflattering, appear as a betrayal of the magnanimous co-operation so liberally bestowed?

Mrs Pandit's own marked capacity for objective judgments soon led

## The Pacemaker 19

me to the conclusion that, if I wrote at all, I must write the truth as I saw it and as such data as I discovered appeared to dictate.

Anything else would be not only a violation of my own standards, but an insult to her intelligence and integrity.

'Difficulties, opposition, criticism—these things,' she once commented to an interviewer, 'are meant to be overcome, and there is a special joy in facing them and in coming out on top. It is only when there is nothing but praise that life loses its charm and I begin to wonder what I should do about it.'

I have not therefore tried to conceal vital events in her personal story or to camouflage the more disconcerting aspects of a diplomat's education—the more so because her own powers of discerning comprehension proved so well able to develop through experience, and in the end carried the trained interpreter of policy right out of the sphere of sycophantic adulation into the realm where the respect of equals begins, and a reputation stands confidently superior to the well-intentioned distortions of uncritical laudation. From this angle Mrs Pandit's career and her ability to accept difficult lessons reflects the comparable experiences of India herself.

Mrs Pandit has stood so long, and so justly, at the summit of world affairs that even if she had no more citadels to conquer, her chief function would remain on record. It has been to create a fresh image of the modern Indian woman, belonging to an old civilization but a new nation, who is thus specially fitted to become a world citizen, with an exceptional understanding of both the past and the future.

CHAPTER I

# An Indian Prison

It was August 18, 1942, and the birthday of the graceful prisoner in Naini Jail, ten miles from Allahabad. Her own years coincided with those of the century.

That morning the prison superintendent had been to see her, though he had not exactly paid a birthday visit. Since insects were everywhere in the hot, humid period of India's monsoon, he had sent her a cane with a leather strap at the end to serve as a fly swat. He now called to ask if it was of any use.

'It helps me to relieve my feelings,' said the prisoner, 'even if I don't succeed in killing many flies.'

'Are you satisfied?' he inquired uncomfortably.

'Would I be in jail if I were?' she replied. He departed quickly, ending their mutual embarrassment. She was left in peace to contemplate the leaking prison barrack half flooded by torrential rain, and the rations left for her after the first two days in which her only nourishment had been a cup of tea supplied by the matron. A quick examination revealed that the food was of the poorest quality, mixed with grit and dirt, tiny stones, and a spider or two for good measure. The minute quantity of ghee (fat) supplied with these unofficial extras was dark brown and smelt peculiar. It was hardly tempting to a prisoner, however hungry, whose food standards were high and fastidious.

Six days earlier Vijaya Lakshmi Pandit had been arrested at 2 a.m. in her Allahabad home by the City Magistrate, the Deputy Superintendent of Police, half a dozen armed khaki-clad policemen and a large number in plain clothes, carried by seven military lorries. This formidable cavalcade was apparently required to overpower one defenceless woman in the middle of the night. Twice before she had been imprisoned, the first time in December 1931 for eighteen months after trial by a magistrate more frightened than herself. She and her younger sister Krishna, also arrested, were transferred to Lucknow Central

## 22 *Envoy Extraordinary*

Prison where the women's section was supposed to provide for juvenile offenders only.

After their release she and Krishna went north with their mother to Mussorie, a hill station in which Vijaya Lakshmi had rented a house for her children and other relatives. This gay, carefree resort was frequented by Maharajahs and their friends who boycotted the rebel Nehrus, though many had been clients of Vijaya Lakshmi's father. Of this visit Jawaharlal Nehru wrote to Krishna from Dehra Dun Jail: 'I fell to musing in a ghostly world of phantoms in which . . . I saw a procession of Rajahs and Ranis and their satellites and parasites dancing away in a veritable *danse macabre*, for they danced on a seething mass of hungry and famine-stricken humanity.'

Vijaya Lakshmi's second arrest, for six months in 1940, had been followed by some vehement protests from England. A letter in *The Times* for December 30, 1940, deplored

'The imprisonment of some of the leading members of the All-India Women's Conference—Mrs V. L. Pandit for example—India's first Cabinet Minister . . . Little information is reaching us of the repercussions in India to these arrests, but the effect on Indo-British relations and on world opinion can be imagined. We cannot convince the world we are fighting for democracy and at the same time maintain this position in India.'

The letter was signed by twenty-six well-known British women— politicians, writers, and social workers, who included Margery Corbett-Ashby, Margaret Bondfield, Vera Brittain, Elizabeth Cadbury, Kathleen Courtney, Margery Fry, Agatha Harrison, Emmeline Pethick-Lawrence, Dorothea Layton, Maude Royden, Edith Summerskill and Sybil Thorndike. A month earlier the *Manchester Guardian*, in a leading article called 'No Progress in India', had made a similar remonstrance.

'Our mishandling of the India problem proceeds according to the most urbane models. The Viceroy has explained to the Indian Legislature with polite regret that we can do nothing more . . . At the beginning of this war we made a mistake for which we are now paying. Out of lack of imagination, which means that we did not understand the India for which we pretended to speak, we declared without consulting her that she was in the war. With more understanding then, we might have had no deadlock now.'

This third time Vijaya Lakshmi was expecting the police, for on

## An Indian Prison 23

August 9, 1942, the nine o'clock evening radio news had announced the arrest of the Congress Working Committee that day in Bombay, following the 'Quit India' Resolution to be passed on August 10th. This Resolution had been the sequel to the rejection by Gandhi of Sir Stafford Cripps's offer of a post-war Constituent Assembly as 'a blank cheque on a failing bank'. Most of the detainees, including Jawaharlal Nehru and Gandhi himself, were now taken to an 'unkown destination' which the British Government kept a close secret from even their nearest relatives.

'Well, it has begun,' said Vijaya Lakshmi, for she knew that a new form of *satyagraha* campaign would follow these precipitate arrests. The family home, Anand Bhawan, became a centre of concentrated activity in preparation for the further imprisonments that were bound to follow, since her niece Indira, Indira's husband Feroze Gandhi, her eldest daughter Lekha, and herself, were all involved. The two younger girls were in the care of a Danish governess, Anna Orusholdt, who had originally come to India as secretary to the famous biologist, Sir Jagardis Bose. Vijaya Lakshmi sent valuables, pamphlets, and all incriminating papers out of the house for safe keeping, and awaited events.

Outside in the streets of Allahabad, the air rang with cries of '*Inqualab Zindabad*' ('Long live Revolution'). Martial law had been established and a curfew imposed. Small boys carrying the orange, white and green tricolour flag of the Congress were taken to the police station and whipped. Peaceful processions and public meetings continued at which the police made mass arrests. For the first time the Pandit girls joined in the protests, while their mother remained at home tense with anxiety for them because the police methods of dispersing crowds were far from non-violent.

A false rumour that one of her daughters had been injured did reacn Vijaya Lakshmi on the eve of her arrest, but when the moment came it was not caused by her concern for them. It seemed, indeed, to be occasioned by nothing more criminal than assistance to a students' procession in which several young men had been shot, and she had helped to pick them up and remove them to hospital. The experience had been both painful and exhausting, and she had fallen into a deep sleep when the police arrived.

Her three daughters, stoical as always though the youngest, Rita, was only twelve, helped her to pack her clothes, and the older girls collected a few books for her to take to jail. Upstairs Jawaharlal's daughter, Indira, lay sleeping after a tiring journey from Bombay; she

## 24 *Envoy Extraordinary*

had been married earlier that year, and was to be taken to prison when still almost a bride. Vijaya Lakshmi, known as 'Nan' to her family, hurried upstairs to leave a few instructions with Indira, and then said good-bye to the girls.

'Don't worry, darling, I'll look after the kids,' Lecky assured her, and Tara promised that they would keep the flag flying. Rita, who had been only two and a half when her mother first went to prison, clung to her for a moment, but spoke firmly.

'Mummie darling, take care of yourself. We shall be fighting the British outside while you are in.'

Later, during Gandhi's 1943 fast, when books and even censored correspondence were forbidden to their mother and Lecky herself was in prison, the younger girls, always resourceful, obtained permission to send Vijaya Lakshmi some tooth-paste, wrapped the newspaper clippings reporting Gandhi's progress round the tube, and then restored it to its container.

Their mother reflected gratefully on their courage as she cleaned some vegetables and cooked them in a *chula* built by one of her fellow-convicts in that portion of the verandah which was to serve as a kitchen. Thenceforward a convict girl called Durgi, of the potter class, would be allocated to help her with cleaning and cooking. This girl of twenty-six had already served eight years for the murder of her husband a few hours after the birth of her baby. Subsequently Lecky helped to take care of this child, and missed her self-imposed task when released from prison.

Durgi was only one of many prisoners sentenced for crimes of violence to whom Vijaya Lakshmi came close during her prison years, but the majority were not criminals in the Western sense; they were victims of social circumstances, imprisoned for minor misdemeanours, rather than intentional wrongdoers. Vijaya Lakshmi and later Lecky studied the prisoners and tried to give them a measure of social insight. The two of them saw in these unfortunates the symbols of all oppression; they themselves represented the victims of an unjust rule, but the convicts were created by an unjust society. Both forms of injustice could be changed, and in so far as Vijaya Lakshmi personally could achieve it, they would be.

In 1942 the prisoners were classified according to their social status by the magistrate, who decided whether they should be 'A' or 'B' class prisoners. This discrimination between fellow workers in a political movement caused much heartburning, and had to be carefully explained by the more fortunate. At this time nothing was done to help

## An Indian Prison 25

convicted persons either in prison or after they were discharged; aid and education for ex-prisoners had to wait for Independence.

When Vijaya Lakshmi discovered that her rations were mildewed as well as gritty, she decided to try to confine herself to bread and tea, though jail tea possessed a lethal quality which she had never encountered outside prison. This time she was at least familiar with the routine and had not to suffer the embarrassments of her first experience, when she did not know how to wash with her clothes on at the public tap, and insisted on having a bucket and cell to herself so that she could take a bath. That procedure seemed a mystery to her fellow-prisoners, experts in washing themselves at the village well.

The only real diversion in prison came from the books that she had brought with her—an anthology of the world's great letters, Gibbon's *Decline and Fall of the Roman Empire*, St. Augustine's *The City of God*, the works of Plato, several volumes on the French Revolution, and India's own great classics, the *Bhagavad Gita* and the *Ramajana*. Three days after coming into prison she had learned, to her great distress, of the death of Mahatma Gandhi's friend and secretary Mahadev Desai, who during his prison life in 1933–34 had written an exhaustive commentary on Gandhi's translation of the *Gita* in Gujarati.

Through reading Vijaya Lakshmi knew that she would eventually acquire the perspective which the times and their challenge demanded. Even now, when she studied the writings of Augustine, or the *Gita*, a symbolic conversation with the soul which she read daily, the City of God did not seem to be far away, for she believed that their costly political adventures could lead to it.

'The man who is able even here on earth, ere he is released from the body, to hold out against the flood-tide of lust and wrath;—he is a *yogi*, he is happy', ran Discourse V of the *Gita* according to Gandhi (the Gospel of Selfless Action). 'He who finds happiness only within, rest only within, light only within—that *yogi*, having become one with nature, attains to oneness with Brahman.

'They win oneness with Brahman—the seers whose sins are wiped out, whose doubts are resolved, who have mastered themselves, and who are engrossed in the welfare of all beings'.

Many Indians, brought up like Vijaya Lakshmi Pandit on the *Bhagavad Gita*,—'God's song' and India's Bible—owed their wider reading to imprisonment. Gibbon's *Decline and Fall* was a special favourite, and Jawaharlal Nehru once announced that, but for prison, he would never have had time to read Oswald Spengler's *Decline of the West*. He might have added that, but for prison, he would not have

26 *Envoy Extraordinary*

had time to write his own famous books, *Autobiography*, and *The Discovery of India*.

Why was this elegant woman, the daughter of a celebrated family with already a distinguished record of her own, enduring for the third time the sordid confinement of a provincial jail? The answer lay in the new 'Quit India' Civil Disobedience campaign initiated by Mahatma Gandhi in his non-violent resistance to British rule after the failure of the Cripps Mission in March 1942. Those imprisoned at this time, a crucial period in the history of the Second World War, were put in jail without a trial and lost most of the privileges which political prisoners had received before.

Outside Naini Prison, with its tense artificial quiet, stretched the endless dusty miles of subordinate India with her huge population—restless, angry, and frustrated. Though the end of two decades of revolutionary strife lay only five years ahead, the goal was not yet actually in sight. But the progress of that struggle had changed the atmosphere of the country and totally transformed those men and women who took part.

Vijaya Lakshmi Pandit's first imprisonment in 1932 had come at a time of acute political hysteria in India; her father, Motilal Nehru, had recently died, leaving the family temporarily rudderless and his colleagues dismayed. Gandhi's *Satyagraha* movement, which Motilal joined late in his life, had been precipitated by the 1919 Amritsar tragedy, which altered the lives of all politically conscious Indians, and affected the country much as the Sharpeville massacre affected South Africa forty years later. In 1921 the British Government had followed Gandhi's campaign with a policy of wholesale arrests.

Two years later these political prisoners were released, but a new sense of unity had come to Indians who had previously thought differently on most national issues, and the next five years proved to be a period of great political activity. Youth Leagues sprang up all over India. During a meeting of the Congress Party in 1929 at Lahore, when Jawaharlal Nehru was President, thousands marched in painfully cold weather to the banks of the Ravi River, and under the clear azure of a winter sky pledged themselves to work for India and total independence. The following March Gandhi started his famous pilgrimage to Dandi, where he broke the Salt Law by picking up salt lying on the sea shore, and released the pent-up emotions of his followers who proceeded to violate the law on a nation-wide scale. In 1931, after the

## An Indian Prison 27

death of Motilal Nehru, Gandhi addressed a huge gathering on the banks of the Ganges at his funeral ceremony.

The Gandhi-Irwin Agreement of 1931 brought a psychological change of atmosphere but did not alter the political picture. During the winter of 1931, while Gandhi was attending the Round Table Conference in Britain, Jawaharlal Nehru and other leaders were arrested. When Gandhi returned to find them in prison, he vehemently renewed the Civil Disobedience campaign, and the movement was soon at its peak.

In January 1932, notices had been served on both Vijaya Lakshmi and her sister Krishna ordering them to refrain from taking part in further meetings. When they attended one in Allahabad on Independence Day (January 26th), they were both arrested and taken to the District Jail, with its diseased women prisoners crowded four to a cell, and the inevitable insects crawling on the floor or slimily penetrating the rough bedding. At their trial Vijaya Lakshmi was sentenced to a year's rigorous imprisonment and a fine, while Krishna, without being fined, received a prison sentence. After four days they were transferred to Lucknow, and Krishna remained in jail for eleven and a half months. For two months even books were forbidden, and they were permitted to have only six saris, to be washed by themselves in cold water throughout the hot, dusty summer. Neither sister could afterwards decide whether the worse discomfort had to be endured during the arid heat, or in the freezing Lucknow winter behind iron bars with no doors to keep out the cold.

The presence of these women in prison was typical of the revolution in the position of all Indian women brought about by Mahatma Gandhi's campaign. The Suffragette movement in Britain had created a concern for social reform in one or two Indian organizations started by a minority of educated women, but it was Gandhi who made a Suffragette movement unnecessary in India. It seemed to him not only deplorable but absurd to organize a national crusade which omitted half the population when the mobilization of the whole nation's brains and vigour was necessary for success.

He brought in the young and immature as well as the older and more experienced; students, both men and women, became politically conscious and organized processions which were fired on by British troops. Members of Youth Conferences were rounded up and put into jail; it was one of these which caused Lecky, at the end of August 1942, to join her mother in prison. There she was known as a 'Q' prisoner (i.e. one who originated in the 'Quit India' movement). She remained in

28 *Envoy Extraordinary*

prison for seven months, in periods of two months which were renewed until she was released. Periodically she and Vijaya Lakshmi read the *Ramayana* together, and she learned to cook on a small oil stove. She lost about ten pounds on the badly-balanced diet, and, never having been ill before, broke out in boils.

In spite of this ordeal, her presence in jail was almost a relief to Vijaya Lakshmi after the mental turmoil caused by repeated partings from her daughters. Later in life, recalling those moments of anguish, she asked herself whether she would ever do again what she did then. Relatives and others, among them her mother, had helped with the children and she had good nurses to take physical care of them, but she knew that life could not have been the same for them as if she had been there. Her daughters when adult told her that these partings had made no difference—or rather, they had led to the development of another and perhaps more valuable type of relationship. But she doubted if she would advise any other young woman to make the same decisions as she had made at that early age.

Through the non-violent techniques of the struggle for independence, Gandhi showed women both young and old a way of escape from hampering traditions within their familiar pattern of life, and gave them a constructive part to play in the rebirth of their country. The great issue of freedom united them with their men. They left their homes for prison and the hustings, and assumed utterly new responsibilities which varied from picketing the shops that sold Western-made cloth to revolutionary speeches at public assemblies. Men and women were all in the struggle together; hence the refreshing absence of sex jealousy when women such as Vijaya Lakshmi Pandit, Raj Kumari Amrit Kaur, and Indira Nehru became prominent. Gandhi started the process which made their careers possible, and their men accepted it.

When the Second World War broke out, the hope of India's rebels that a new nation might arise from international chaos seemed at first to be destined for disappointment. Without her consent, India was declared a participant; it appeared that the old-style colonialism still dominated the thinking of British leaders. The total change of outlook which came with the Labour victory of 1945 seemed more like sixty than six years away. India, keenly deploring the European dictators, was not even allowed to mobilize her resources under her own commanders on the side of the Allies.

Torn between her sympathy with Hitler's opponents and her hatred of imperialism, India begged for a declaration of Allied war aims, but received no reply. The most Congress could do was to send medical

## An Indian Prison                                    29

units to the front at the time of the Japanese invasion and receive Jewish refugees fleeing from the Nazis, while their own Ministers resigned in protest. In 1942 they angrily rejected the half loaf of promised freedom 'after the war' in the belief that British promises, usually hedged about with conditions, were never kept, and emphasized their indignation by the new Civil Disobedience movement. This comprehensible scepticism was to bedevil the sincere and patient work of Lord Pethick-Lawrence and his colleagues in the Cabinet Mission of 1946.

In 1940 Gandhi had started the policy of individual *Satyagraha*, choosing Vinoba Bhave as his first volunteer. The second was Jawaharlal Nehru, who almost immediately found himself in Dehra Dun Jail sentenced to four years' imprisonment. This ferocious sentence stunned all India, and not least the two Nehru sisters to whom their handsome, dynamic elder brother had seemed a pillar of strength. He was now fifty-three, and faced what appeared to be a remaining lifetime of continuous imprisonment. So psychologically close to him was especially Vijaya Lakshmi, that his frustrating and seemingly interminable fate filled her with a helpless exasperation almost equal to his own, though this was controlled. He himself had written to Krishna that 'going to jail is a trivial matter in the world today, which is being shaken to its foundations'.

Thenceforth Vijaya Lakshmi shared Jawaharlal's idealism, and when they were separated she had an intuitive understanding of the way that his mind was working. But all through the Civil Disobedience movement her love and admiration for him overwhelmed her personal judgment; until his death he possessed her consciousness more than any other man, including her husband. In later life when she would have to make political judgments she learned to think independently of him, though she was always influenced by her awareness of his wishes which normally coincided with her own.

In August 1942 not only Jawaharlal but other members of Vijaya Lakshmi's family were in prison; they included her husband, Ranjit Sitaram Pandit, her sister's husband Raja Hutheesing, and for a short time Krishna herself, though the care of two very small sons obliged her to avoid continuous involvement in the national struggle. In those apocalyptic days, moments of exultation alternated with moods of sorrow and frustration. The solitary prisoner, cut off in Naini Prison from communication with her family and the outside world, inevitably experienced both.

What kind of woman was this embarrassing rebel, who had been Swarup Nehru and was now Vijaya Lakshmi Pandit? Her mobile

# 30 *Envoy Extraordinary*

mouth and lustrous brown eyes bore witness to a quality of generosity which her daughters many years afterwards were to describe with warmth. Whenever she travelled she brought back so many gifts for friends and relatives that jealous opponents accused her of extravagance. Added to this quality was a capacity for home-making which transcended the restrictions even of prison, where every mat was given its function and basically unattractive meals made tolerable by the way she served them.

She would always be ready to acknowledge her share of the characteristic family faults which she and her brother possessed in common —a quick temper; intolerance of fools and blunderers; and impatience with the inept creators of disappointment. But with the impatience went an even larger share of the family charm. In her own eyes her best assets were the God-given quality of being able to make and retain friends, and the power of adaptation to many varieties of persons and surroundings. To this she might have added her keen love of life, and her interest in everyone she met.

Above all, this prisoner was pre-eminently herself, but like the rest of humanity she was the product of her heredity, her family, and her environment. Contrasting with the squalor of an Indian prison barrack, the bright pictures of her specialized upbringing were cast as by a magic lantern upon the sensitive screen of her mind.

CHAPTER 2

# A Prisoner Remembers

SWARUP NEHRU, Motilal's elder daughter, who later, at marriage, changed her name to Vijaya Lakshmi Pandit,[1] had been born in a great mansion called Anand Bhawan ('Abode of Happiness') in the European quarter of Allahabad, a pleasant city with 260,000 inhabitants in the United Provinces, now Uttar Pradesh, some ten miles from her present less agreeable location. Once known as Prayag, it was regarded by Hindus as holy because it stood at the meeting place of two sacred rivers, the Ganges and the Jumna, and the Emperor Akbar had renamed it 'the abode of Allah'.

Later the city was to become somewhat shabby and derelict, but in Swarup's childhood it had been a place of gracious homes and carefully tended gardens, with a tranquil atmosphere contributed by the university and judicial courts. Its dominating personalities were then such famous lawyers as Sir Tej Bahadur Sapru, Pandit Madan Mohan Malaviya, and Swarup's father Motilal Nehru. All these three, and several of their colleagues, could command high legal fees at this period, described in a February 1962 BBC broadcast on Jawaharlal Nehru as 'the long hot imperial afternoon'.

These fees made possible the purchase of Anand Bhawan, a white rambling bungalow-shaped house with an immense garden, bought in 1899 when Jawaharlal was ten. With its small domed turret and three tiers of verandah screened by delicate lattice work and supported on the first and second floors by narrow columns, it suggested a richly-decorated ship poised high in the water. When its owner joined the national movement in 1921 this huge house was re-named Swaraj Bhawan ('Abode of Freedom') and used for Congress Party offices and a free dispensary, while three-quarters of it remained unoccupied and silent. Motilal built a smaller Anand Bhawan across the roadway from the old one, but the birth-place of Swarup was the first magnificent home in which her parents had then lived only for a year.

[1] See p. 41.

# 32        *Envoy Extraordinary*

At that time Lord Curzon, another lover of grandeur and then the undisputed ruler of a sub-continent, had reigned for three years as Viceroy, and in the midst of sprawling, over-crowded, poverty-stricken Calcutta, had built himself a Government House, with a vast garden and artificial lake, modelled on the family seat at Kedleston in Derbyshire. Crowds visited the Nehru's comfortable home every year from the multitudes that came to bathe in the sacred rivers or attend local religious feasts. As they were too large to control, they were allowed to distribute themselves over the compound, and rest.

In her dingy prison barrack without amenities, the former Swarup, now Vijaya Lakshmi Pandit, recalled the household possessions and treasures which she was to describe years afterwards in a broadcast on her brother, India's first Prime Minister: the big stable with its many horses; the new car which they were the first Indian family to possess; the big indoor swimming pool which had been a source of pride when such pools were rare, but was left to gather cobwebs after the Congress Party had taken over the house. Forcing herself to eat her unappetizing rations from cheap, coarse dishes, she pictured the richly-cooked meals exquisitely served on beautiful Dresden and Sèvres china, the Irish linen napkins, and silver candlesticks on the table decked with flowers in the English fashion.

Swarup's father had been a benevolent despot cast on noble lines who adored his family. His birthday fell on the same day, month and year as that of Rabindranath Tagore. He belonged to the Kashmiri Brahmins, aristocrats in the complex caste structure of Hindu society, who for centuries had lived lives dedicated to public responsibilities, and were thus naturally authoritative in outlook and manner. Two hundred years or so earlier, an ancestor of Motilal named Raj Kaul had left his province to seek his fortune in Delhi, where the Moghul court was established. About 1716 this Sanscrit and Persian scholar had been granted a house in the capital, and the word 'Nehru', from *nahur*, a canal, was added to his name. After the mutiny of 1857 his descendants scattered over the United Provinces, and adopted the local languages of Hindi and Urdu. Behind them, in Jawaharlal's words, lay 'hundreds of passionate generations'.[1] In spite of these lofty origins, Motilal was self-made in the sense of possessing no inherited wealth, but he atoned for this deficiency by the millions of rupees that he both earned and spent as a highly successful lawyer.

He spoiled his two daughters, of whom the younger, Krishna, was born seven years after Swarup, but, strangely enough, he never had

---

[1] From a letter to Krishna Hutheesing quoted in *With No Regrets*.

# A Prisoner Remembers 33

them trained for any profession, though they were taught to shoot and to master other masculine skills. There was even talk about a University and the Bar for Swarup, but in spite of his enlightened outlook nothing came of it since he regarded marriage as a woman's first objective. Even in her youth her unfinished education, carried out at home and afterwards in Switzerland by a series of governesses, left her with a sense of deprivation for which she sought to compensate by uninhibited but disorganized reading in her father's library.

In later life she never admitted to any early literary ambitions—'probably because of my haphazard education in which no one was interested'—but expressed herself easily on paper, and from the age of fifteen wrote with enjoyment for Hindi periodicals. Years afterwards she compared the slight effort always demanded by the preparation of her able speeches with the easy technique of her Wellesley-educated daughters.

Motilal belonged to a generation of Indian intellectuals brought up to admire and even imitate the British Raj; he took Swarup to England when she was five and provided her with an English governess. This governess, finding too unfamiliar the nickname 'nanhi' (the little one) habitually given to the first daughter in a Kashmiri household, compromised by calling the child 'Nan'. Even the family accepted this name, and in later life it was used habitually by Vijaya Lakshmi's more intimate friends.

Long afterwards Sir Grimwood Mears, who was Chief Justice in the Allahabad courts when Motilal practised there, described him as 'a delicious person' with 'all the brains that the best good fairy could have given him'. Motilal remained unmoved by the type of Indian nationalism based on the Hindu religion which was characteristic of nineteenth-century India, and had little use for Hindu religious and social customs. Throughout his life he broke down barriers of prejudice and caste, though he, like Gandhi, could not accept his teen-age daughter's subsequent desire to make an unorthodox marriage. In spite of this clash of strong wills, Motilal remained her ideal and the dominant influence in her early life.

'I was closer to my father than anyone', she once replied to a London journalist who questioned her on their relationship. Long-standing friends of the family have stated that it was she, rather than her brother, who resembled their father in temperament and character.

In the painful year 1919–20 after the Jallianwalla Bagh massacre at Amritsar, Sir Grimwood remained, as he himself testified, 'the only Englishman that Motilal loved to see'. For it was the events at Amritsar,

C

# 34 *Envoy Extraordinary*

when Britain's General Dyer ordered his troops to fire on an Indian political demonstration, killing 372 Indian citizens and wounding thousands in an enclosed square from which they could not escape, which completely changed Motilal's outlook in common with that of many cultured Indians. Another influence was that of the poet Mrs Sarojini Naidu, who wept when she spoke of Amritsar in London in 1920 at Muriel Lester's East End settlement, Kingsley Hall.

'My sisters were stripped!' she cried. 'They were flogged; they were outraged.'

It was several months before the British Government, which subsequently denied Mrs Naidu's accusations, reprimanded the trigger-happy General whose precipitate action was to prove a new starting point in the making of a nation; they even permitted him to accept £50,000 raised for him in a fit of benighted patriotism by the *Morning Post*.

'It is vain to expect justice from a race so blind and drunk with power,' Mrs Naidu wrote bitterly to Gandhi. Motilal decided that further co-operation with Britain was impossible, joined Gandhi's nationalist movement, and thereby profoundly influenced the whole Indian intelligentsia.

The younger Nehru, now aged thirty, had pledged himself to this movement some years before Amritsar. When Gandhi returned from South Africa in 1916, Jawaharlal had been one of the first to answer his summons. Motilal had then not wholly approved, and many arguments between father and son had disturbed the atmosphere of Anand Bhawan. Now Motilal, with characteristic thoroughness, decided at the age of sixty to break completely with his former life.

He gave up his lucrative practice at the Bar, sold his horses and carriages, cut down his legion of servants, kept only one cook instead of two or three specializing in different varieties of foreign cuisine, and substituted coarse *khadi* for his fine Western-made clothes. Even his cellar of choice wines went with the rest, since Gandhi was teetotal, and with them he sold much of the precious china and glass in which their food and drink had been served. His wealthy professional acquaintances began to fall away, as such fair-weather friends tend to do, when his friendship no longer meant attractive luxuries but a demand for personal sacrifice and the adamant repudiation of still powerful rulers.

'To understand,' his grand-daughter Tara has written, 'how a man with an epicure's enjoyment of life could, at the age of sixty, quietly give up the luxury in which he had indulged ... is to understand a fraction of the mind of a nation bewitched by Gandhi.'[1]

---

[1] Nayantara Sahgal, *Prison and Chocolate Cake*. London, Gollancz, 1954.

## A Prisoner Remembers 35

Motilal remained equally unshaken by desertion and criticism. In 1921, when the Prince of Wales was visiting India and decided to include Allahabad in his itinerary, the District Magistrate requested him to put his grounds at the disposal of the royal guest. Motilal refused to allow the use of Anand Bhawan for this purpose, though as a non-co-operator he promised to see that the Prince suffered no harm. For this refusal Motilal was arrested and sentenced to six months' imprisonment by an embarrassed local Magistrate. Subsequently he was twice elected President of Congress.

Swarup had never felt so close to her mother, Swarup Rani, who represented the Eastern, and traditional, side of the household. No Western influence had affected Swarup Rani, a devout Hindu; when she married at fourteen she had no thought but that of conformity with the old pattern of a devoted wife and mother quietly functioning in the background and exercising, in so far as she could, a moral influence on her family.

'She was responsible for our knowing what we do of, really, the roots of Indian life', Vijaya Lakshmi once said in a broadcast.

Her grand-daughters, who called her 'Nanima', remember Swarup Rani as a tiny, beautiful woman, with the hazel eyes and fair complexion characteristic of the Kashmiri, and small well-shaped hands and feet which contributed to her appearance of a delicate Dresden china doll. When the girls visited her on Sundays at Anand Bhawan, her attitude towards them was one of amused tolerance rather than demonstrative affection. Persistent ill-health—she barely survived the birth of Krishna—had added an impressive sharpness to her manner. Nayantara Sahgal writes of 'her helplessness and pampered beauty', but also records that, with incongruous gallantry, 'Nanima' gave up her rich clothes and luxurious comforts, and in late middle age courted imprisonment and arrest, after Motilal had joined Gandhi.

Throughout her life she was devotedly served by an early-widowed sister, Bibi Anima, known to the children as Babima. When Swarup Rani eventually died from a stroke, Babima, killed by shock, followed her within twenty-four hours. Every Sunday she had given the Pandit daughters their lunch cooked in her simple kitchen, and told them fairy-stories of which the plots showed an unlimited capacity for invention that any sophisticated modern novelist might envy. To Nayantara the death of this kindly great-aunt represented her first overwhelming loss.

In 1961, when Ludovic Kennedy asked Vijaya Lakshmi in their BBC interview whether she had always got on well with her brother, she replied judiciously to this leading question: 'We came together when

## 36 *Envoy Extraordinary*

we started working together in politics'. This period began after the death of their father.

As a child she had in fact seen little of Jawaharlal, for he was eleven years her senior, and at the age of fourteen was sent to school at Harrow and then to Trinity College, Cambridge, until 1910. He took a degree in Natural Science, and continued with two years' study as a barrister in the Inner Temple. In the 1962 BBC broadcast of his life, 'Man of Two Worlds', a London surgeon, Mr Hugo Romanis, recalled the small unassuming Indian boy, known to his fellow undergraduates as 'J. Nehru', who had come up to Cambridge from Harrow in 1907. 'J. Nehru' made his earliest impression by becoming cox of one of the First Trinity boats in the Lent races; his quiet unfanatical insistence that India must ultimately belong to the Indians was to make a greater impression much later.

Swarup first became really conscious of him when he returned to India in 1912, a hero to his two small sisters, and a lover of winter sports, swimming and riding. In his *Autobiography* he assessed the Cambridge arguments on human problems as 'all make-believe'; during those pre-First War years the time had not yet come when he and the elder of his sisters would realize with shame and sorrow the contrast between their comfortable lives and those of the naked, starving and miserable multitudes of India. Yet the first unhappy intimation of racial politics made its impact on Swarup when she was only thirteen.

One day she was galloping in the Mall at Simla during a visit when an elderly British resident, annoyed by the noise of her horse's hooves, struck at it with a whip while exchanging acid remarks with his wife about 'those damned natives'. Taya Zinken, who related this episode in *The Guardian* for July 28, 1961, justly added: 'It was this type of "education" which gave its sense of inevitable crisis to the Amritsar tragedy.'

Seven years later, when Swarup married, she found a close and affectionate comradeship which proved to be wholly satisfying, and much easier than the often baffling relationship with her brother. Jawaharlal, supersensitive to potential accusations of nepotism, appears always to have been reluctant to mention her publicly or to acknowledge her services. Her name does not appear at all in the Index to *India's Foreign Policy*, the massive collection of his speeches on the subject published in August 1961, though his comment in a speech on Non-Alignment (December 4, 1947) and on the part played by India at the United Nations—'I should like to pay a tribute to our delegation,

## A Prisoner Remembers

especially to the leader of the delegation'—must have referred to her.

Vijaya Lakshmi shared with Ranjit Sitaram Pandit the type of experience familiar in our generation to women who lost a young lover in war, but later knew happiness with a husband who brought friendship and affection rather than passion into their lives. Ranjit, she once said, always held that her greatest quality was her ability to talk with him as though she were a man. They were married for twenty-three years and in her opinion he taught her nearly everything she knew, for he co-ordinated her knowledge instead of conveying unrelated fragments of miscellaneous information.

When Ludovic Kennedy followed his question on Jawaharlal by asking whether her marriage had been 'arranged', she denied the suggestion vehemently. At thirteen, according to an article by her sister Krishna Hutheesing in the *Ladies' Home Journal* (USA) for January 1955, she was formally engaged to a somewhat priggish young man from a well-known family. Her tradition-dominated mother, rather than her father with his respect for Swarup's intelligence, had set her heart on this match. It was not, however, the young man's commonplace character which finally brought the abortive arrangement to an end, but, in her sister's words, 'her desire to marry another' whose background then seemed incompatible with the needs and outlook of the national movement.

Mahatma Gandhi himself helped her through this period of grief and frustration; he took her to stay with his wife Kasturba and himself at their ashram in Sabarmati, a forty-eight hours' journey from Allahabad, and thereby established the deep respect and affection which she felt for him to the end of his life and beyond.

When she returned her anxious father, to whom she was so close, warmly forgave her for her part in the crisis which they had shared, and the family went to Kashmir for the summer. It was then that the famous cobra incident occurred for which Krishna Hutheesing is again the authority.

On a warm May afternoon the family was resting on the grass near a stream when Motilal looked up from his book and to his horror saw a huge King cobra rearing itself over Swarup, who was also reading. Quietly her father said: 'Nan, don't stir. There is a cobra near your head.' She raised her eyes and, though paralysed with fear, managed to keep still. The others held their breath until the cobra, neither attacked nor frightened, slid peacefully away.

That evening a beggar, who had learned of the incident through

## 38 *Envoy Extraordinary*

India's incredible grape-vine, called at the Nehrus' camp. He told Motilal that this alarming threat had been a wonderful portent, for it meant that Swarup would rise to great heights and become very distinguished. Her personal story, he added, would not be very happy. This prophecy proved to be strangely near the truth, for beneath the shining surface of her official life would always be a deep undercurrent of private sorrow.

Shortly after the holiday in Kashmir, Ranjit Pandit, a barrister from Kathiawar, came to Allahabad to consult her father. There he met her, and proposed marriage within two or three days. In a radio talk early in 1939, when she was a Cabinet Minister in the Provincial Government of the United Provinces, the former Swarup Nehru described this decisive event.

'In November 1920 I met for the first time the man whose wife I am. That day stands out in my life. My children sometimes ask me what chance brought a man from far Kathiawar to marry a daughter of Kashmir. To this question I have no answer save that the chance was a lucky one. This period is vague—seen now dimly through a veil.

' "Will you marry me?" he said. "I have come many a mile and crossed many bridges to come to you, but in future you and I must cross our bridges hand in hand."

'We were married on May 9, 1921—a critical and difficult year for a couple to launch on the sea of matrimony. There have been many ups and downs in our life—some of the bridges we have had to cross were shaky, they threatened to give way, but always we have gone over together and, even after eighteen years, I can still be glad for that day in November when we first met each other.'

Ranjit Sitaram Pandit, like his uncle S. P. Pandit, the orientalist, was a true scholar who spoke eleven European and Indian languages. A Sanskrit specialist, he translated Sanskrit classics into English; one of these was Kalhana's *Rajatarangini*, or 'The River of Kings', which Jawaharlal Nehru asked his sister Krishna to send him in February 1943 when he and Ranjit were both in prison. This document was a history of Kashmir, and one of the few historical works in Sanskrit.

Ranjit was also outstanding as a musician; he had a good singing voice, played the violin, and was passionately addicted to both Eastern and Western music. He also loved outdoor life, and especially riding, swimming and gardening; his 'green fingers' brought bright patches of colour even to the drabness of a prison yard. With all his talents he was laughter-loving and gay, bringing north the gaiety of Western India,

## A Prisoner Remembers 39

the land of Indian chivalry. His daughter Tara describes him as nearly six feet tall, with a bronze skin and thick hair, curly and black. Recalling his contemplative eyes, sensitive hands, and the strong chin of a quick-tempered but determined man, she states that he was for her 'the human being nearest my heart'. In *Prison and Chocolate Cake* she publishes a picture of him which shows a tall debonair figure, with his hands in his pockets, and a smiling youthful face with laughing eyes. He is wearing a brocade dressing-gown, casually flung on and tied with a tassell, and a pair of flat, loose-fitting sandals.

The Pandit family came from a village called Bambuli, on the Ratngiri coast of Bombay province. Ranjit's grandfather Sitaram had studied law in London; he and his wife then left Ratngiri for Kathiawar, at that time a complex pattern of princely states dominated by British influence.

In his youth Ranjit, handsome as a young prince, absorbed the lively Kathiawar folklore and dances. He received the best education that Western India could provide, going first to Bombay University, and thence to Christ Church, Oxford, and the Middle Temple. His father, a leading Rajkot barrister with a large practice and a princely income, was pro-British and had put his other sons through the India Office, but Ranjit refused to take that direction; instead he spent four years obtaining degrees at the Sorbonne and Heidelberg University.

After this spectacular education he married at twenty-nine, which was late for an Indian, and eventually settled with Vijaya Lakshmi in the United Provinces. Thus their daughters were brought up in their mother's Kashmiri tradition, and spoke Hindi and Urdu rather than Marathi. If he had wished for a son the girls never knew it; the West of India gave women more freedom than the East and North. He had grown up detesting the 'purdah mentality', and believed that girls should have the same education and opportunities as boys. The fever of nationalism caught hold of him soon after his marriage, but this was not surprising since he shared his West Indian background with Gandhi. His father had been for a time Gandhi's *guru* (teacher and guide), and a close friendship had developed between Ranjit and Jawaharlal Nehru.

Now, in 1942, this political purpose meant prison for them both, and the disruption of family life so early that when Vijaya Lakshmi first went to jail her daughters were still so small that they were allowed to go straight to her prison barrack, and remembered the shock, even at that age, of seeing their mother, always so elegant and associated in their minds with rose-decorated verandahs, wearing coarse *khadi* in

# 40 Envoy Extraordinary

dismal surroundings. Many of their acquaintances thought her crazy to adopt this unattractive attire for the shibboleth of freedom, just as Ranjit seemed to them utterly insane to throw away the financial security of a flourishing law practice and the scholarly life he loved for a wild political ideal.

Because she could now see him only for brief intervals in jail, his wife sometimes solaced herself with mental pictures of their shared life at Khali, the family's summer home high in the Kumaon hills nine miles from Almora, inaccessible by train, and for some years by car. Now they could drive there through evergreen forests where tiny blue and white violets jewelled the mossy banks. She thought of their evening suppers on the porch where they watched the sunset cast a sanguine glow over the Himalayan snows, and afterwards sat beside the crackling log fire over which she read to the girls from the *Ramayana* which told them of their long heritage.

None of them had realized, in the early summer months of 1942, that the family were together at Khali for the last time. Afterwards it was there that Ranjit's daughters most clearly remembered him, with his sun-tanned face and laughter on the wind. But their mother's mental pictures went further back, and she sometimes recalled their splendid wedding in May 1921.

It was the first of three weddings which contributed to her personal kaleidoscope. The second, her sister Krishna's to Raja Hutheesing in 1933, had been in sharp contrast to her own, for Krishna's future husband was a member of the Jain community from Gujerat, and as a Brahmin she could marry him only by civil registration. As her mother, three years a widow, was too ill to insist upon a religious ceremony also, Krishna and the tall gentle stranger who was taking her away to live in Bombay were quietly married in the family drawing-room without any of the traditional ritual.

The third wedding, that of her niece Indira, Jawaharlal's twenty-five-year-old daughter, to Feroze Gandhi,[1] had also been celebrated at Anand Bhawan, in March 1942.

Indira's wedding was a simplified version of the usual long ceremony, and had lasted only for one and a half hours. At this function Indira had worn a shell-pink *khadi* sari woven from yarn spun by her father and edged with silver embroidery. Tara, who left on record a description of the dress, recalled also that Vijaya Lakshmi's eyes uncharacteristically filled with tears as she watched this ceremony; the reason, perhaps, was the empty mat beside Jawaharlal on the floor where Indira, dark

[1] He was not related to the Mahatma.

## A Prisoner Remembers 41

and beautiful, with delicately moulded features, sat facing him according to custom. The mat would normally have been used by her mother Kamala, who had died in Switzerland in 1936. But perhaps, thought Tara, the cause of Vijaya Lakshmi's sudden emotion was the forlorn shell of Swaraj Bhawan across the garden wall, and the memory of her own wedding in the vanished fairy-tale world of twenty-one years ago.

Swarup Nehru's wedding had been celebrated with traditional magnificence at Anand Bhawan, though with respect for the new national movement she wore a *khadi* sari instead of the customary silk, adorned only with fresh flowers which replaced the rich jewellery that normally decorated an Indian bride. Mahatma Gandhi himself had been present, and her wedding garment had been woven from yarn spun by his wife Kasturba. On that day she changed all her names at once, since a Hindu bride is renamed by her husband's family; from Swarup Kumari Nehru ('Beautiful Princess') she became Vijaya Lakshmi Pandit ('Goddess of Victory').

The marriage ceremony, lasting for hours, had followed the traditional pattern, with hundreds of guests and a fabulous trousseau consisting of 101 saris, and rich accessories of bangles, armlets, and anklets in gold, which Motilal's lavish taste preferred to silver. Her wedding gifts had included furniture and silver utensils for the new home, as well as a car and a horse. No one then pictured the demure little bride, her stormy passions resolutely subdued, seated at her parents' feet with her gold-braided hair fastened above her neck by jewelled pins, as the future rebel, and much less the future Ambassador. After their marriage she and Ranjit began their life together in Calcutta, where he had joined the High Court, and she followed the practices of every well-to-do young married woman, with visits to the British Club, and to British friends who organized expeditions to the races and polite games of tennis.

But the pattern soon changed, for shortly before her wedding Gandhi had launched his *Satyagrahi* campaign, and though the Nehru family, so soon to symbolize in themselves the Indian struggle, had not yet put themselves behind it, Vijaya Lakshmi realized even then that it was bound to affect her life. Before the year ended the British Government had begun its campaign of wholesale arrests, and the young wife, who had been brought up to think well of Britain and its people, had now to unlearn her admiration, though she was to insist years later that it was the colonial system and not the British people which she began to criticize. With those British who were soon to be working in England for Indian independence she was always wholly

## 42 *Envoy Extraordinary*

at one, and would include many of them among her best friends for the rest of her life.

These friends of India had their own difficulties, partly due to the official obscuring of the lives and fortunes of leading Indians when the Second World War began. In his Introduction to Krishna Hutheesing's autobiography *With No Regrets*, Professor Amiya Chakravarti called this negative propaganda 'the blind mist which has been deliberately created to blacken the most sacred reputations'.

After Ranjit had joined the Freedom Movement he and Vijaya Lakshmi left Calcutta and returned to Allahabad, now the centre of the new nationalism, where they lived near her parents in a house with dark green shutters and a garden adorned by large trees and a rose-bordered lawn. Like Vijaya Lakshmi, as she often reflected gratefully, the women of India had joined Gandhi in large numbers, leaving their sheltered homes, speaking in public, going to jail, taking up political and social work, and thereby not only serving the national movement but destroying their own tabus. With very few exceptions their men, like her husband and brother, and Raja Hutheesing and Feroze Gandhi, had supported their claim to equality and independence.

Twenty years afterwards, in the televised film portrait of her brother, Vijaya Lakshmi Pandit summarized in retrospect the effect of these changes on her family:

'Suddenly Anand Bhawan and all that it had meant became meaningless and, in fact, terribly superficial. . . . Everything pertaining to the past was put away, and we began to live an austere life. . . . So the whole approach to life changed in Anand Bhawan, and not only a new approach to life, but a new awareness of ourselves and of India came into the picture which had never been there before.'

CHAPTER 3

# Family in Revolt

VIJAYA LAKSHMI'S earliest contact with Gandhi had occurred in 1915, when as fifteen-year-old Swarup Nehru she had been taken to that year's sessions of Congress, and thus first experienced the influence which years afterwards, in the words of a London correspondent in Denmark, was to give to her judgment of political problems 'a certain great-minded sensitivity'.[1]

Four years after that Congress session, as a girl of nineteen described by Eleanor Morton in *Women Behind Mahatma Gandhi* as 'a perfect Kashmiri beauty', she and her sister had attended a parade in Bombay against the Rowlett Acts.[2] At this protest meeting Gandhi spoke, supported by the brilliant and voluble Muslim lawyer Mohammed Ali Jinnah, and by Mrs Sarojini Naidu, then forty-two, who later was to campaign vehemently against co-operation with Britain, and in 1924 to become the first Indian woman to be President of Congress. Motilal had sent his limousine to fetch Gandhi, and Swarup drove with them through gardens vivid with pomegranate palms and hibiscus to the mosque where the gathering was held.

After this meeting Motilal withdrew all his objections to Gandhi's *Satyagraha* programme. He gave his son, now thirty, permission to join it, and thus began to make his family into the dynamic group which for almost half a century was to draw to itself the vital political and social developments of a sub-continent.

When Krishna, then only twelve, asked the Mahatma: 'Why don't you wish us to fight the British, Mr Gandhi?' he explained quite simply the new technique which was to liberate India—'an aggressive yet non-violent method of resisting those who wished to do ill'.

On April 6th, the day of a *hartal* initiated by Gandhi on which everyone stopped work, the Amritsar massacre occurred. Instantly

[1] Paul Palmer in *Extrabladet*, February 1960.
[2] Measures initiated by a Committee presided over by Judge Rowlett, which proposed to control 'subversive' behaviour by giving judges power to try political cases without juries.

# 44        *Envoy Extraordinary*

India was aflame; Gandhi began the publication of the paper *Young India*, and became his country's leader. Two years later, when the Prince of Wales, twenty-seven, charming and gay, visited India, riots preceded his arrival, and when he entered Bombay with his colourful retinue of native Princes, the streets by Gandhi's orders were deserted.

So violent was the revulsion in India that when the much-revered Annie Besant, who had been President of Congress only a few months earlier, opposed Gandhi's attitude on Amritsar, she was repudiated as a British partisan, discarded as a leader, and left India in May never to recover her former prestige.

In December of that year 1921, Motilal and Jawaharlal, with many others, came before the District Magistrate and were sentenced to six months' imprisonment. Two years later all the political prisoners were released, and Motilal became President of Congress after the death of C. R. Das. In 1926 Vijaya Lakshmi and Ranjit accompanied Jawaharlal and his wife and daughter Indira, then aged nine, to Switzerland, and the year after, Motilal himself followed them to Europe.

Following India's rejection of the Simon Commission in 1928, great activity began among the politically-minded. Congress was held in Calcutta that year, and its members again elected Motilal President. It was now a completely revolutionary organization, which had moved very far from its origins, of partly British Liberal inspiration, in 1885 as 'a loyal opposition to H.M. Government'. The earlier tension between Motilal, then supporting Dominion status, and his son who wanted complete independence, had totally disappeared. The alien imperial rule had been splendid, dutiful, and even by its own standards sacrificial; it had modified many excesses of Indian religion and family custom, and had left thousands of its own dead in India's dusty earth. But the subject people had now outgrown the stage of being overawed and impressed, and Motilal, with India, was ready to challenge Britain's authority.

In 1929, when the Congress met at Lahore, Jawaharlal was elected President. By now, though to the end of Gandhi's life Jawaharlal was to find him visionary and impractical, he wholly accepted his leadership, seeing him as the patron saint of their country's freedom and the originator of a new type of revolutionary campaign.

'Gandhi gave us some particular training,' said Indira in a broadcast long afterwards, 'and he stressed the fact that we must not be bitter in any way and that our struggle was not against English people but against the system.'

Vijaya Lakshmi too subsequently recorded his effect upon her at an

## Family in Revolt 45

early age on the first occasion that she heard him address a public meeting in Allahabad and ask for funds.

'I found myself struggling to pull off some gold bangles I had on my wrist so that I could put them into the bag when it came. And I just got a few off by the time the bag came. Afterwards I couldn't think why I'd been so moved. But he had this quality of magic about him.'

Though she had been associated with the developing All-India Women's Conference throughout the nineteen-twenties, Vijaya Lakshmi's political work actually began when, with her sister-in-law Kamala, she organized a boycott of British goods among the women of Allahabad. At the age of thirty she emerged from the cloistered life of an aristocrat, and started to picket the shops selling foreign cloth.

During that year Jawaharlal was again arrested and sent to Naini Prison. His imprisonment was a severe shock to Motilal, who vigorously returned to civil disobedience, and on June 30th was arrested himself. Though an 'A. Class' prisoner he had to eat prison food and keep all the rules, with no special amenities, and his health rapidly declined. In January 1931 Jawaharlal, with Ranjit Pandit who had also been arrested for taking part in a salt *satyagraha*, was released, and with Gandhi visited his father. During Motilal's last illness he continually asked to see Ranjit.

The following month Motilal was taken to Lucknow for X-ray treatment, and there died on February 6th in the Kalakander Palace. Crowds followed his body back to Anand Bhawan, where it was taken to the banks of the Ganges for the burial ceremony. Gandhi and Pandit Madan Mohan Malaviya addressed the crowd, who vowed themselves to work for India's freedom.

'It was this for which he gave his life,' said Gandhi of Motilal, and revolutionary India went into mourning for two days. On Friday 21st Jawaharlal wrote in self-dedication to his sister Krishna: 'As every day passes I feel his absence the more and a terrible loneliness takes hold of me. But we are children of our father and have something of his great strength and courage, and whatever the trials and difficulties that may come our way we shall face them with resolution.'[1]

During these momentous years the three Pandit daughters had been born, in 1924, 1927, and 1929, and their father chose their names—Chandalekha ('Crescent Moon'), Nayantara ('Star of the Eye') and Rita Vitasta ('Truth'). In the climate of the time, and in the family to which they belonged, the years before them offered a combined prospect of high adventure and bitter heartache. Asked by Ludovic

[1] *Nehru's Letters to His Sister*, London, Faber, 1963.

# 46 *Envoy Extraordinary*

Kennedy in her 1961 interview whether they had suffered from their separations from her due to her imprisonments, Vijaya Lakshmi replied: 'Of course, of course ... I've had many moments of anguish about my family, and wondered whether I'd do again what I did then, of abandoning them more or less to fate.' She might have quoted a revealing passage written on March 17, 1943, and included in her diary *Prison Days*: 'I feel torn in two between my duty to the children and the other duties of serving the country which, in our case, has come to mean long months of imprisonment.'

But the three girls, like most intelligent young people such as many of the British children who confronted the risks and terrors of the Second World War, faced their fate with a positive, philosophical acceptance. In her broadcast interview their mother added: 'My daughters tell me now that it's made no difference, and that there was another kind of relationship developed between us later.' She must have derived much comfort from Tara's assertion many years afterwards that she and her sisters were truly the children of Gandhi's India, 'born at a time when India was being reborn from an incarnation of darkness into one of light'. They grew up with India into political maturity—'a different kind of political maturity from any that the world had seen before, based on an ideology inspired by self-sacrifice, compassion, and peace.'[1]

To begin with the girls were brought up by a series of governesses, who kept them on a strict regime of boiled vegetables, custard puddings, regular walks, and early bed. But before their mother's first imprisonment in 1932, when the portents of future happenings were becoming unmistakable, they were sent to a boarding school in Poona. In 1935, when Vijaya Lakshmi was a member of the Allahabad Municipal Board, they went to live with their uncle at Anand Bhawan.

After college at Lucknow, a period of prison, and education in the United States where she studied Political Science, 'Lecky' was destined to become a journalist, working on the Lucknow *National Herald* until her marriage. She married an Indian Government foreign service official shortly after her mother's period as Ambassador in Russia, and travelled with him to posts in Chungking, Paris, Vienna, Pakistan, and Goa. Nayantara began in her twenties to make her name as an author, while Rita accompanied her mother to the United States in 1945. All three girls, as might be expected, became unusually good-looking, and owing to their father's stature, considerably taller than their mother. Rita, like her eldest sister, married an Indian Government official.

[1] *Prison and Chocolate Cake*, 1954.

## Family in Revolt 47

Nine months after Motilal Nehru's death in January 1931, Jawaharlal was again arrested on a journey from Allahabad to Bombay. Two days later Gandhi, who had been in London attending the Round Table Conference, returned to India. Finding Jawaharlal and other leaders in prison, he began the fight for freedom again. Congress supporters joined in widely, and even Motilal's fragile widow began to address meetings in fiery speeches which astonished her family.

After their release from prison in 1933, Vijaya Lakshmi and her sister went for a time to Calcutta, where Jawaharlal's wife Kamala was ill. Little has been recorded of Kamala; her life, said a friend of Krishna's, was like 'the luminous flame of an oil-lamp.'[1] Frail and child-like, she nevertheless joined the women volunteers at 5 a.m. each day, and at 8.0 started picketing the shops selling foreign cloth. She retained a girlish sweetness to the end of her life, which came all too soon. Her health deteriorated fast from 1934 and she went to Switzerland, seen off by her husband who was then in Almora Jail. Later he was temporarily released, and flew to Europe to join her. She died in Lausanne on February 28, 1936, with Jawaharlal and nine-year-old Indira beside her.

In 1934 a new type of experience began for Vijaya Lakshmi; she turned her attention to the far-reaching reform programmes needed in India, and stood successfully for the Allahabad Municipal Board as a Congress candidate. The following year she was elected Chairman and served on the Board for two years, in which she laid the foundations of her skill in public speaking. To begin with this was an ordeal; in 1953 she admitted to Stanley Burch of the *News Chronicle* that her first speaking engagement found her facing a vast audience without an idea in her head. Then, she added, 'suddenly something happened. The crowd before me became part of myself. We were both part of some bigger unseen force'. Later she learned to treat the crowds as friends, each member to be addressed individually.

At that time she had still no thought of any major part in inter-national affairs; though her support of the All-India Women's Con-ference pointed to a political future, her work on the Allahabad Board involved the social and humanitarian preoccupations habitually regarded in public institutions as the special (and sometimes exclusive) functions of women. She made, however, a far-sighted endeavour to convert the existing night schools into real literary centres, and to model the evening institutes on Soviet principles adapted to Indian needs.

A contribution made by her about 1936 to a contemporary feminist

[1] Krishna Hutheesing, *With No Regrets*, Bombay, Padma Publications Ltd., 1944.

# 48 Envoy Extraordinary

symposium[1] dealt with 'Children and Their Upbringing', and concerned itself with such traditional 'women's topics' as children's health, meals, bed-time, physical education, and imagination. But the essay displays more than a modern attitude towards these practical subjects worthy of the pioneer Chelsea Babies' Club; it also shows an enlightened conception of the obligations of parenthood which at that time and place was peculiarly her own.

'Here (in India) we are apt,' she wrote, 'in our excess of respect for the old, to neglect the young. We expect our children to grow up and serve us as we have been taught to serve our elders. . . . How utterly wrong this is. . . . Our children are not born to serve us—it is we, rather, who should serve them, for the future is theirs. . . . Children are individuals with definite rights; and those who would train them must first train themselves.'[2]

In 1935 came the Government of India Act, introduced as the result of recommendations from a Joint Committee of Lords and Commons set up by Britain's National Government after the Round Table Conferences had failed. This Act established full Provincial autonomy with responsible Ministers, subject to limited 'reserve powers' vested in Provincial Governors, and General Elections followed in 1936. The Congress Party went into these elections, which marked its first experimental co-operation with the Government 'in its appraisal of the various political parties', in order to test its own standing in the country.

Vijaya Lakshmi and her husband both put up for election in the United Provinces, and the elder girls returned for their first holiday from Woodstock School (an American-owned boarding school) to find their parents deeply involved. Vijaya Lakshmi's constituency was the rural district of the nearby city of Kanpur, known as the Cawnpore Bilhaur area, and Ranjit's was even nearer—a district across the river from Allahabad known as Jumna-par. Vijaya Lakshmi's opponent was Lady Srivastava, the wife of the (British selected) Minister of Education in the UP Government, and the only woman member of the old Assembly. The supporters of Congress, unlike those of the rival parties, could not afford to pay for transport. Humbly and enthusiastically,

---

[1] Our Cause. A Symposium by Indian Women. Edited by Shyam Kumari Nehru, Allahabad, Kitabistan, about 1936.
[2] This concern for children remained a lifelong preoccupation. The World's Children (Save the Children Fund publication) for September–October 1953 records that Vijaya Lakshmi became the Honorary Secretary of India's first 'Save the Children' organization, an All-India Committee which in 1951 formed the nucleus of the present Indian Council for Child Welfare.

## Family in Revolt 49

regarding the election as a pilgrimage, they walked immense distances to cast their votes for the Pandits and other Congress candidates. The elections produced a Congress majority in seven out of the eleven provinces of India. Both the Pandits were returned, and Vijaya Lakshmi announced her victory to her daughters in a telegram: 'Yes for Mummie.' In spite of the peculiar difficulties of her contest against her woman opponent, she had won with a majority of 10,000 votes in a constituency numbering about 38,000 men and women voters. The following summer she was elected unopposed as Minister of Local Self-Government and Public Health for the United Provinces, where the Premier was Pandit Govind Vallabh Pant. A tall man with a drooping grey moustache and twinkling eyes, he was eventually to become Home Minister in Jawaharlal Nehru's Cabinet and survived until 1961.

Vijaya Lakshmi's photograph went all over India as that of the first Indian woman, and the second in the British Empire, to become a Cabinet Minister.[1] During her term of office she piloted the Panchayat Raj Bill, which revived the old institution of the Village Council after a lapse of two hundred years and gave the villagers wide powers of self-government. The United Provinces (Uttar Pradesh) was the first province to place this Bill on the Statute Book, and all the present village reforms in India arise from it. Thus, ten years before she began to present the 'image' of Indian diplomacy to the outside world, she contributed substantially to the welfare of the humble men and women for whom Gandhi and her brother had always been so much concerned.

Almost immediately Vijaya Lakshmi had also to face a severe cholera epidemic, which smote the foothill area of Harldwar where 6,200 people died and three million were threatened. She tackled the emergency with courage and resourcefulness, touring cholera-stricken and famine-ridden areas as no Indian woman had done before her, and organizing medical assistance from many miles away. This work was ultimately to send her to England to study British methods of public health, for her opposition to colonialism never deprived her of appreciation for her opponents' methods. She also made herself responsible for many Jewish refugees fleeing to India from Hitler's Germany.

In spite of these serious responsibilities Vijaya Lakshmi remained her elegant self, dressed always in spotless Khaddar and Swadeshi garments, and unfailing in her love of beauty and order. A short book, *So I*

---

[1] The first was Margaret Bondfield, Minister of Labour in Ramsay Macdonald's 1929 Labour Government.

D

50 *Envoy Extraordinary*

*Became a Minister*, which she wrote soon after this appointment, described her first inspection of the ministerial office where so much of her time was to be spent.

'There was a large writing table in the centre of the room, and an equally large leather-covered sofa against the wall. The rest of the space was occupied by innumerable chairs, small tables and book-shelves, and looked like a second-hand furniture dealers' shop. A perfectly impossible pink carpet struck a discordant note against the apple-green distemper on the walls, and layers of dust covered everything. I stood in the doorway and surveyed the room with a sinking heart. How could I sit here and concentrate on important matters?'

So she had the pink carpet removed; a few pleasant compliments to the old caretaker produced a more tolerable example in beige and bluish-green. The awkward angles of the writing table and sofa were changed, the superfluous chairs and book-shelves banished to the storeroom, and some restful blue-green curtains from her own home hung against the windows. Finally she demanded flowers, preferably roses. When her secretary expressed alarm at this innovation, she showed signs of intending to cut the flowers herself, and he quickly provided them.

This concern for her working environment was to accompany Vijaya Lakshmi throughout her life. As Governor of Maharashtra in 1963, she decided to change the enormous official desk in the Raj Bhawan in Bombay. It certainly suggested billiards rather than private conversation, and put an intimidating and unnecessary space between the Governor and her visitor.

Before long Vijaya Lakshmi's name had become a legend all over the United Provinces; her autographed picture was in constant demand, children were named after her, and she was inundated with letters. Of this fan-mail she once said: 'The Indian temperament exceeds in emotionally worded epistles, which keep one in suspense as to what the aim of the writer is, until one has waded through a sea of beautiful metaphors to the final paragraph.'

She also became accustomed to journalistic interviews, and found the female questioners more exasperating than the male; they insisted upon asking her opinion on clothes, children, and petty social activities. When one London journalist asked if she never felt inclined to do 'ordinary things about the house', she replied innocently that she enjoyed these as much as more distinguished activities. Next day the

## Family in Revolt 51

article appeared under the headline: 'Indian Woman Minister darns husband's socks.'[1]

It was not surprising that she often envied her brother the straightforward intelligent questions usually asked him about his work. During this period her daughters normally spent their school holidays with her in Lucknow, and on April 22, 1938, Jawaharlal wrote to Krishna of their home at Allahabad:

'I live in Anand Bhawan as a guest almost, and I feel relieved that the burden of keeping house is not upon me. Nan, specially since she became Minister, has also got more and more wrapped up in work, although, of course, she is not quite so much of a political animal as I am.'

If this comment and the added 'of course' had once been true they did not long remain so; the dedicated organizer of security and discipline soon learned to adjust her double allocation of gifts without sacrificing either.

At the beginning of that year she and her brother and sister lost their mother, the small woman like an exquisite Kashmiri doll who was only five feet tall but had not feared to experience the dust and heat of the revolutionary campaign. Swarup Rani died from a third attack of coronary thrombosis on a night when Vijaya Lakshmi was about to travel to Lucknow by a midnight train; she fell suddenly as she rose to embrace her daughter, and died before morning. She and Motilal had lived together for nearly fifty years.

[1] From Padmini Sen Gupta, *Pioneer Women of India*, Bombay, Thacker, 1944.

CHAPTER 4

# The Cost of a Crusade

VIJAYA LAKSHMI enjoyed her Provincial Ministry as much as anything in her career for it was creative pioneer work, but like all her colleagues she resigned in 1939 when the British Government declared India a participant in the Second World War without consultation. She did not return to office until 1946, when the Attlee Labour Government was in power in Britain, and the Simla Conference of May 5th–12th had been held by the Cabinet Mission. Its members, Lord Pethick-Lawrence, Sir Stafford Cripps, and Mr A. V. Alexander,[1] had been sent to India to prepare the path to independence.

In December 1944, Vijaya Lakshmi was to explain their 1939 resignation policy to a representative of the *New York Post*. Its meaning, she said, could not be clearly understood

'unless one understands the background of events leading up to the outbreak of war. Granted that Gandhi is a pacifist by tradition and conviction, but the truth of the matter is that the Congress Party ... had made repeated requests to combat Fascism—not only as early as Japan's attack on Manchuria in 1931, but as far back as the beginning of the rise of Fascism in Italy, in the twenties. But at every step our efforts were thwarted. Is it any wonder, then, that having been consistently denied the opportunity to fight for the larger issues at stake, India should have been thrown back into fighting for what one might call the smaller issue—namely, its own independence?'

Jawaharlal responded by rejecting the war, which in the circumstances he regarded as no proper concern for a dedicated nationalist. He was no more ready to compromise in war than in peace, and was prepared to accept a British defeat if that meant independence. For him, and for all the Congress leaders, this was a foreign war. That year Muriel Lester, the friend of India who had stayed at Gandhi's ashram and had been his hostess at Kingsley Hall in 1931, frankly told her acquaintance Leo Amery, the Secretary of State at the India Office:

[1] Later Earl Alexander of Hillsborough.

## The Cost of a Crusade 53

'India is not bluffing; she will not aid the Empire without being assured of independence.'

At this period Ranjit Pandit was writing to his puzzled daughter Tara: 'We do not want to see the spread of triumphant Hitlerism. We stand for freedom, peace and progress. We are against wars to destroy the freedom of weaker nations by violence and force. If England is in favour of the freedom of the nations then she must not forcibly occupy India and keep the peoples of India in bondage. Freedom must not mean freedom for European countries only; such freedom must be for all countries including countries in Asia and Africa. If the British Government are willing to agree to this, then Indians may co-operate with British to establish a new and better world.'

For a time the Indians hoped that, from the chaos engulfing imperialism, a free India would arise, but no declaration of war aims came to encourage the subject millions who had looked for a change of heart. Thus it was that in 1940 Gandhi started individual *Satyagraha* once more. Though Jawaharlal and Sir Stafford Cripps were friends and fellow Socialists, he had refused to compromise on the suggestions made by Sir Stafford at the time of the Cripps Mission in 1942. The British Government now began to look on Jawaharlal as a menace which could not be tolerated in wartime, so on a journey from Wardha to Allahabad he was 'spirited away', taken to Gorakhpur for trial, and sentenced to four years' rigorous imprisonment.

Vijaya Lakshmi was now a sponsor of the All-India Women's Conference, with its constructive programme for the civic and political rights of Indian women. From 1940 to 1942 she became its President, and was also elected a Vice-President by the Women's International League for Peace and Freedom, but found herself unable to establish effective relations with women supporters in England owing to the regulations by which they were themselves restricted.

Her own third period of imprisonment now loomed ahead. The vindictive sentence imposed on Jawaharlal shook his sisters more than any of his previous relegations to jail. In her essay 'The Family Bond', in *A Study of Nehru* edited by Rafiq Zakaria, Vijaya Lakshmi included her recollection of his trial on that occasion:

'There is one memory which never leaves me. It was soon after the breakdown of the Gandhi–Irwin Pact. Bhai had been arrested, taken to Gorakhpur, tried and sentenced to four years' rigorous imprisonment. My husband and I were at the trial which, as usual, had ingredients that Gilbert and Sullivan could have used to advantage. After the trial the

# 54        *Envoy Extraordinary*

prisoner was led away from the court-room across the road to the jail. We were permitted to go and say good-bye. He was his usual self, full of assurance about the benefits of a jail term, the speed with which time rushed by, and humorous messages to the younger members of the family. As we walked away, I turned back for a last look. He stood against the sun which was setting in a great orange ball behind his head. He held the bars on either side, and the face so recently full of mirth was serene and withdrawn, and there was infinite compassion in the eyes which no longer saw us. He was already deep in his own contemplation.'

In spite of the implications in lost time and opportunity of this new term of imprisonment, he was able to write from prison to Krishna: 'I have seldom felt so peaceful in mind as I have done lately. Through some practice I have learnt to draw myself in and shut the various drawers of my mind which relate to activities which have been suspended ... Physical work and suffering are after all petty compared to the troubles and tempests of the mind.'

His dreams, added Krishna in *With No Regrets*, were all woven round the future of India—'an India in whose coming greatness Jawahar has not the shadow of a doubt and in whose service Jawahar would gladly lay down his life.'

In January 1941 Ranjit Pandit had joined his brother-in-law in jail for a short period, and Jawaharlal reported: 'Ranjit and I are here by ourselves.' Ranjit, he wrote, was busy translating an old Sanscrit play, the *Madrarakshasa*, written about the seventh century during the Gupta period. 'This is a political and historical play dealing with Chanakya and Chandragupta's time and is full of the wiles and intrigues of kings and their ministers. The world has not changed very much after all.'

In his *Autobiography* he recalled that in jail Ranjit had begun to teach German to Pandit Malaviya; he also related that those in prison were often strangely detached, and could view calmly and dispassionately the scene in which they were both in and out, feeling that petty individual errors and weaknesses mattered little 'when vast forces were at play and the mills of the gods were grinding'.

'This was the time,' commented Patrick O'Donovan, the narrator in the 1962 broadcast, *Man of Two Worlds*, 'that turned a nationalist into a statesman. Prison did for him what Cambridge could not do. It completed his development as an Indian leader.'

Similar experiences turned the older of his sisters into an Indian

# The Cost of a Crusade 55

leader too. In her television interview with Ludovic Kennedy twenty years later, she spoke of the lessons she had learned in prison: 'for those of us who had never had the opportunity of going to college or university, it really was the university of life.'

But at the time those valuable lessons which would mean so much for the future were less apparent than the odious forms of life which crept, crawled and flew about the damp and derelict prison barrack. In *Prison Days* Vijaya Lakshmi's diary for August 19, 1942, describes the experience of getting out of bed suddenly and putting her foot on a large toad. On another occasion after her daughter had joined her in jail, an outsize bat fell from the roof right on Lekha's chest.

'We were much too frightened to sleep after that. Who says prison life is lacking in thrills?'

More usual examples of unwelcome intruders were mice, ants, tiny black gnats, and mosquitoes. Their humming disturbed the quiet of the night, which would otherwise have been a relief from the perpetual noise of argument and quarrelling by day, and the sound of young boys being thrashed on the other side of the yard. An October entry in her diary recalls the words of Francis Bacon: 'For a crowd is not company and faces are but a gallery of pictures and talk but a tinkling symbol where there is no love.'

Behind the physical discomforts lay the worse torment of perpetual anxiety about her family. Lecky's arrival in jail had left Tara and Rita alone in Anand Bhawan, constantly surrounded as it was by police and CID men. Of Ranjit she had received no news since he left for Bombay three weeks earlier.

'I wish,' she wrote, 'I could communicate with him to tell him to be careful about his health. Not knowing Bhai's (Jawaharlal's) whereabouts is also worrying me.'

On September 19th Ranjit was arrested at Anand Bhawan directly he returned from Bombay. Vijaya Lakshmi's diary reveals a growing deep concern for him, as though she possessed a subconscious knowledge of the new tragedy so soon to descend on them. An entry on September 11th just before his arrest shows her fears to have been fully justified.

'Ranjit has been very unwell and could not leave Bombay ... I am terribly worried about Ranjit. He wants such careful looking after.' On the day of his arrest she added: 'He returned from Bombay the night before last. Poor Tara and Rita! I was hoping they would have at least a week with their father. But in these days man proposes and the British Government disposes.'

56                    *Envoy Extraordinary*

On October 16th she recorded in her diary that she had lost six pounds in weight since her admission to jail on August 12th.

Typically Ranjit sent her some seeds and cuttings to grow in the prison yard, and at their fortnightly interview brought her a bunch of vivid nasturtiums. In his *Autobiography* Jawaharlal describes how during one of their early jail experiences in Naini Prison, Ranjit created a carpet of gay flowers in their dismal enclosure and even laid down a miniature golf course.[1]

Ranjit now continued calmly to work on a translation of the *Ritusamhara*,[2] and at one interview severely scolded his wife for nearly breaking down when she was forbidden to see thirteen-year-old Rita, who had come all the way from Anand Bhawan in the hope of getting a glimpse of her mother.

'Do you mean to tell me you actually asked permission to see Rita?' he said. 'Haven't I told you again and again that we cannot seek favours from these petty *gauleiters* who are placed in authority over us! You mustn't let your feelings get the better of you. You are too big a person, my dear girl, to ask favours from anybody. There is no room in this struggle for softness or favours. Pull yourself up.'

She did, and in May 1943 was recording her deep consciousness of unity with him and the comfort he brought her. 'I am sometimes amazed at the sense of oneness I have with Ranjit and yet how many years we have spent apart.'

For a being so keenly conscious of the value of human affections, the uncertain fate of Jahawarlal, who so often disappeared from her ken behind official bars, was another constant source of pain. Just before his fifty-third birthday in November 1942, when the seventeen years of his great authority were still nearly half a decade ahead, her diary recorded her love for him.

'Out of the many good things fate gave me at my birth, one of the best was surely my brother. To have known and loved him and been so near to him would have been ample justification for being born. In a few days it will be his birthday—another birthday spent in prison. So many good years of his life wasted—I feel very rebellious when I think of all he has had to go through.'

The last entry in 1942, for December 31st, found her speculating with good reason on the uncertain future.

[1] Jawaharlal Nehru, *An Autobiography*, London, John Lane, 1936, p. 239.
[2] A description of the six seasons by Kalidasa. This work was in the Press at the time of Ranjit's death.

## The Cost of a Crusade    57

'What does 1943 hold for us, I wonder? More sorrow and suffering or a glimpse of the promised land? Whatever it is, I pray we may face the future with courage and dignity. My thoughts turn more than ever to the little ones alone in Anand Bhawan. But I am confident they will conduct themselves worthily, and that thought helps.'

The immediate future was to show her how well justified had been this confidence in her children. For some time the idea had been growing in the parents' minds that if the education of the two elder girls was to be appropriately completed, they ought to go to college in the United States in spite of the risks involved by wartime travel. As they had attended Woodstock School, American methods of education would not be unfamiliar to them.

In *Prison and Chocolate Cake*, Tara explains clearly and with evident agreement their parents' reasons for sending them away. From August 1942 the renewed non-co-operative movement had been in full spate; the political atmosphere was tense and unsuited to study, and education itself surrounded by restrictions. It was also subject to drastic interruptions; Lekha's college terms had already been divided by seven months' imprisonment. She had been intended for Oxford, but in 1941, the year that she would have entered, England had been under constant attack from the air, and Britain's position in the war was still grave two years later. Thanks also to the British Raj, thousands of men and women of all ages were in prison throughout India, and Vijaya Lakshmi and Ranjit did not want their daughters, to whom for political reasons they had been unable to give the normal childhood they desired for them, to study in a vast concentration camp. The United States was still almost untouched by the war and there they could live free from perpetual crises.

During their brief interviews in jail, the mother and father made preliminary plans to send their elder daughters away. In March, owing to an illness which followed the period of anxiety caused by Gandhi's 'fast unto death' from February 10th until early in March, Vijaya Lakshmi was allowed out of prison on parole for thirty days, and went to Anand Bhawan where Krishna joined her for a week. The house was dark and silent; servants no longer hurried to and fro; only one dim oil lamp in the porch and another in a bedroom penetrated the gloom.

Krishna, in *With No Regrets*, has described their meeting. In her room Vijaya Lakshmi rose to embrace her, and Krishna noticed how much her sister's comely face had changed in a few months. Vijaya Lakshmi herself wrote in her diary that she felt like some Rip van

## 58 *Envoy Extraordinary*

Winkle returning after decades to haunts once familiar but now unrecognizable.

Before she went back to jail, she discussed with Lekha the parents' plan of sending her and Tara to Wellesley College. Lekha was reluctant to leave India and argued against the scheme, but finally agreed to go. Her mother cabled friends in the United States—one being Madame Chiang Kai-Shek, herself a Wellesley graduate—to arrange for the girls' admission. Within forty-eight hours a reply came from the College President: 'Wellesley College proud and pleased to welcome your daughters.'

Though friends and relatives criticized this courageous scheme, Vijaya Lakshmi was encouraged not only by Ranjit's whole-hearted support but by the agreement of her brother.

'My immediate reaction was in favour,' he wrote to Krishna of the scheme from Ahmednagar Fort on April 30th, 'and the more I have thought of it, the more I have liked it . . . As for risk or possible danger involved in the journey, that surely cannot and should not be a reason against the proposal. To my mind it is an inducement in favour of it. We have never made "safety first" our motto and I hope we never will. In this world full of risk and danger we must take our share of them and not shirk them. It would be bad training indeed for the girls to be made to feel they must avoid risks and dangers at all costs.'

A fortnight later he added:

'It amuses me to learn that people unknown to you and the girls are writing to you to express their disapproval of their going. I should not worry much about this, unless I was myself of that opinion. It is astonishing how people constitute themselves the judges of other people's private lives and activities, without ever troubling to understand those other people.'

On April 19th Vijaya Lakshmi saw her daughters off to Bombay, and drove straight back from the station to Naini Prison.

'The parting was a difficult affair,' she wrote next day in her diary, 'and though we were all very near to tears we would not give in and kept talking of other things . . . I know we have done the right thing in sending them to the United States. They will have wider opportunities of development and will be well cared for and yet . . . and yet . . . America is so terribly far away.'

In her book Nayantara has described their previous parting with their father, who made the occasion as cheerful as he could. She swallowed her tears, and Ranjit laughed and teased as usual. With the

## The Cost of a Crusade 59

permission of the Superintendent, a jovial Anglo-Indian, they even sang songs together in the prison, drowning the sound of its persistent gong. Ranjit assured them that going to America was nothing to worry about though no one else seemed to approve of it. The only advice he could give them, he said, was to enjoy their new life. They left him, grieving that his superb intellect and vital energy were wasting behind prison bars. But these separations, Tara later commented maturely, did not spoil the relationship between children and parents but created a new world of values. She might cry for her mother in secret but never doubted the rightness of Vijaya Lakshmi's procedure. Family life was imbued with a deep sense of unity and shared ideals, and the times spent together were all the more precious because they were so rare.

At Bombay the girls were seen off on an American troop-ship by their aunt Krishna, who did her best to conceal her apprehensions, and found themselves among fifty regular passengers and seven hundred Polish refugees. The possibility of submarine attack stimulated rather than alarmed them;[1] nor were they perturbed by the unexpected route of the ship, which took them via Australia through a wintry climate for which their mother, to her subsequent alarm, had not provided. Their eventual arrival at San Pedro in California was equally unexpected, and equally disturbing to their parents, since their friend Mrs Frances Gunther, the wife of John Gunther, was awaiting the girls in New York, three thousand miles away.

But Lecky and Tara, who had made friends on shipboard, were totally undismayed by their predicament. A fellow-passenger fixed them up for a week in a Los Angeles hotel, where the hotel detective took further care of them, and nothing disturbed them except the fact that nobody they met seemed ever to have heard of India. When eventually, seen off by the detective, they arrived in New York, America's characteristic hospitality and kindness enveloped them.

The majesty of New York—so spectacular a contrast to Allahabad —exhilarated them both, and they soon learned how to accomplish the unfamiliar domestic tasks for which no household workers had been

---

[1] In *Testament of Experience* (1957) I wrote of my son and daughter—almost the contemporaries of Tara and Rita—that they had grown to adolescence during the Second World War 'constructing their own patterns of life in an age not merely of catastrophe but of wonder; a century of opportunity in its fullest and deepest sense. Watching them, I perceived that to be born into an apocalyptic era may be a cause for rejoicing rather than lamentation; the problems to be resolved demand, and create, spiritual resources which the prosperous ease of a golden age will never inspire'.

Lecky and Tara provided evidence, like my own John and Shirley, that the youth of this revolutionary epoch grew up to develop for themselves the positive qualities required to meet its challenge.                                                                                    V.B.

60 *Envoy Extraordinary*

available in America since the War began. They proved brilliantly equal to luncheons with Mrs Roosevelt and Mr Wendell Willkie, and even conducted two Press conferences with an assurance which suggested that such events had been weekly occurrences in their young lives. The only shadow on their exultant happiness was the thought of their parents in prison.

Vijaya Lakshmi, for all her heartache, need not have worried about them; their exceptional parents had brought them up to be fully self-sufficient. She had better reason for her deep anxiety about her husband, as the coming months were so grievously to prove. The closing pages of *Prison Days* are shadowed by her growing concern for him.

'I am told,' she wrote on April 27, 1943, 'that men deternees of the first class will be sent to Bareilly in a few days. I hope Ranjit will not be transferred to Bareilly jail. In 1932 this place broke his health completely. It is a notorious place and in his present condition it will immediately affect Ranjit. As the summer comes he grows weaker and has been having trouble with his breathing again—I can't bear him to be in prison. He is so much a child of the wide open spaces.'

Six days later the announcement of Ranjit's transfer to Izatnagar Central Prison, Bareilly (UP), came through. In her distress at the news Vijaya Lakshmi hardly thought of her own loneliness when deprived of their periodic interviews. 'I hate the idea of Bareilly,' she recorded. 'I am sure Ranjit will be miserable there . . . He is not meant to be in the rough and tumble that is Indian politics. With his wealth of learning and fastidious scholarship, his love of art and of all those finer aspects of life which are understood by so few people, this association day after day with crudeness and ignorance is breaking him down physically. It is a slow daily sacrifice which can be so much more deadly than some big heroic gesture made in a moment of emotional upheaval . . . I can only hope for the best and trust that Ranjit's tremendous will-power will help to keep his mind and body fit.'

A further entry on May 11th explained the peculiar disadvantages of Bareilly Central Prison, surrounded by a twenty-five-foot wall which reduced the hours of sunlight available for reading and writing, where the temperature periodically rose to 110°.[1]

'It is badly located and is known as one of the worst prisons in the province. When Ranjit was there in 1933 he fell very ill owing to the

---

[1] Describing this prison in his excellent book *Nehru. A Political Biography* (Oxford University Press, 1959), Michael Brecher has recorded how adversely it affected Mr Nehru's own health in the Spring of 1932.

## The Cost of a Crusade 61

place being constantly filled up with smoke from a neighbouring factory. It took months of careful nursing after his release to build up his health.'

By June 4th she was painfully awaiting a letter from him. The constant anxiety for his welfare, and for that of her daughters who had sailed on May 15th and were now on the Atlantic, undermined her own health in the mounting summer heat. On June 11th she recorded that she had been unable to leave her bed for several days, and was shortly to be released.

But Ranjit was not set free until October 8th, when his health was rapidly failing owing to the onset of pleurisy. In spite of this threat he visited Allahabad and Bombay and went up to Khali, perhaps with an intuitive awareness that he was seeing his beloved Almora home for the last time. On November 8th he returned to Lucknow, where he was still a member of the Legislative Assembly, and stayed with a friend, Colonel G. R. Oberai of the Indian Medical Service.

Very soon his illness worsened; his release had come too late for the treatment he needed to take effect. Though she hurried to Lucknow, even his wife's devotion had not the power to save him. Now she would never be able to tell him that the chequered history of their family, with its brilliant lights so often dimmed by black shadows, had been destined for a triumphant ending after all.

At five o'clock in the morning of January 14, 1944, he experienced a sudden acute difficulty in breathing. An hour later Ranjit Pandit, the lover of literature and learning, was gone, a willing but incongruous martyr to the cause of his country's freedom.

CHAPTER 5

# Courage in Herself

————◆◆◆————

RANJIT had never sought the limelight; absorbed in his books, manuscripts and music, he was content to leave this dubious asset to his wife and brother-in-law. But after the news of his death had spread across the United Provinces, Lucknow University closed for the day, and crowds from all over Allahabad came to the Pandit house to await the coming of the bier after its 100-mile journey from Lucknow.

Late in the afternoon Vijaya Lakshmi and Rita, with Indira and Feroze, arrived at their home. Jawaharlal, held in prison, could not be there, and was compelled to endure his grief for a beloved relative alone within the inhospitable walls of Ahmednagar Fort, 'a Moghul relic in a remote corner of Bombay Province,'[1] 700 miles from his family in Allahabad. Two famous lawyers, Sir Tej Bahadur Sapru and Mr P. N. Sapru, called on Vijaya Lakshmi, and at about 5 p.m., with Ranjit's body beneath a tricolour flag, the funeral party left the house for the meeting-place of the Ganges and the Jumna rivers, where his ashes were scattered.

Shortly afterwards Mahatma Gandhi sent Vijaya Lakshmi a message.

'People will come to condole with you, but I shall not sorrow for you. How dare I pity you? One does not sorrow for the daughter of a courageous father, the sister of a courageous brother, the wife of a courageous husband. You will find courage in yourself.'

That courage, helped by her daughters, she was soon to discover. They had heard of their father's death on a cold January day while staying in downtown New York with a married couple named Elly, from Boston, and Ruzzack, from South India. 'There was no place in America,' Tara recorded in *Prison and Chocolate Cake*, 'where we would rather have been at that time than in this house of loving and wordless sympathy.' To Vijaya Lakshmi they sent a cable. 'Be brave, Mother. He can never die. He lives in us.'

[1] Michael Brecher, *Nehru. A Political Biography*, p. 288.

## Courage in Herself 63

Tara's own need for courage came most acutely after the coming of Independence, when she returned to a home and an India without her father, whose life the struggle for freedom had taken.

'Never again,' she wrote seven years afterwards, 'should I see him walking in the dew-wet grass of early morning as he loved to do, a brown Kashmir shawl thrown over his white, khadi-clad figure. Never again should I be able to talk to him of books and music, of stars and trees and people, of the thousand things he had taught me to understand.

'It was ironic that he had to go, my gallant, laughter-loving father, to whom life was adventure . . . but a subject India had chosen him to serve among her martyrs, and it was a prison, the symbol of all that was opposed to his nature, which had claimed him in the end . . . Bitterness filled me that he had to die, till I remembered that bitterness had been his most scorned enemy . . . To bow before it now would be to deny all he had lived for and the purpose for which he had died.'

Three weeks after Ranjit's death, Jawaharlal wrote with resolute philosophy to his sister Krishna from prison.

'My mind has been trying to adjust itself to the fact that he is no more. That is not easily done, and yet sometimes I feel that ages have passed since he died. But adjustment has inevitably to be made . . . Every death upsets the equilibrium not only of various individuals but of the group or groups of family and friends. There is a gap. That gap remains and yet nature establishes a new equilibrium.'

It was this equilibrium which Vijaya Lakshmi had now to seek, and she sought it with a determination inspired by her own basic vitality. On February 17th she replied to a letter of sympathy from Agatha Harrison, the Quaker friend of India who at that time was continuously working with the India Conciliation Committee set up by the Society of Friends to seek a way out of the tension between India and Britain.

'Ranjit's passing,' Vijaya Lakshmi wrote, 'was sudden and unexpected. We were beginning to hope he had turned the corner. I can never think of him as dead. You know how perfect the bond was between us. He was my comrade in the fullest sense of the word and my ally on the battle-fronts of life. I shall be alone without him but not lonely because for me he will continue to live in all the beautiful memories he has left behind. My girls have been wonderful and their splendid courage gives me the strength to carry on. They are as fine as their father and I have much to be thankful for. I am trying to take up the threads of life again and get back to work.'

64 *Envoy Extraordinary*

When we have lost our chief source of stability and consolation, the only comfort which is both immediate and constructive comes from the possibility of serving others who are carrying a similar burden of grief and perplexity. At this time the service was needed by India herself, first within the country, and secondly in the wider world. In this Vijaya Lakshmi found anew the courage that Gandhi had known her to possess.

An early opportunity came in Bengal, tragically smitten by famine since the previous year. War 'priorities', bureaucratic failures, the self-interest of Indian traders, and finally the loss of Burma with its rice-fields, had created a serious shortage of consumer goods. Inflation followed, with famine on its heels. During 1943 and 1944, it was officially estimated that $1\frac{1}{2}$ million persons perished and another $4\frac{1}{2}$ million suffered gravely from malnutrition in one of the century's worst calamities. Men, women and children fell dead outside the wealthier homes of Calcutta; the corpses of others covered the muddy tracks of Bengal's many villages and the fields of her rural areas.

In helpless anguish Jawaharlal Nehru contemplated this spectacle of pointless misery from his distant prison, and in *The Discovery of India* recorded his bitterness and frustration:

'Men were dying all over the world and killing each other in battle ... Death was common enough everywhere. But here death had no purpose, no logic, no necessity; it was the result of man's incompetence and callousness, man-made, a slow creeping thing of horror with nothing to redeem it.'

Though he was bound, his sister at a great price was now free; she hastened to Bengal to organize relief in the stricken areas and set up centres for the famine orphans. The British Raj, moving with its customary monumental lethargy, belatedly recognized its responsibilities thanks largely to the masterful initiative of the new Viceroy, Lord Wavell; and adequate relief measures were at last begun.

By this time Vijaya Lakshmi had her own acute problems to face, for she learned that Ranjit had died intestate; he had departed suddenly, and, in spite of his failing health, his love of life and beauty had perhaps been too strong for death to appear an immediate threat. Under Hindu law as it was then established a widow could not inherit; nor had Vijaya Lakshmi a son who could carry on an estate received from his father. Everything that Ranjit had possessed went back to the family of his elder brother and, after a life of safe economic prosperity, she now faced the threat of actual penury.

## Courage in Herself

Financial provision for the education of the two older girls had been officially secured at the time they left India because their parents were in .prison, and Lecky had further help as the first holder of the Mei Ling Soong Scholarship established at Wellesley by Madame Chiang Kai-Shek for an Asian student.[1] But Vijaya Lakshmi had herself to maintain and a teen-age child to support. Had she ever been tempted to give way to grief, she had now to recognize that it was a luxury which she could not afford. Nor could she listen to the jealous, ill-natured gossips for whom she had always been a target. When she broke her first juvenile engagement, conventional Indian society had called her a 'bad girl'; then the critics said that she would leave her husband or he would leave her. Now they speculated how soon she would marry again, since she clearly did not intend to fall back upon the emotional retreat from life and responsibility customary in Indian widowhood.

She decided to go to America, support herself by lecturing, and thus act as the persuasive spokesman for the cause of Indian freedom which her country needed abroad. Gandhi himself urged her to go, and seeking an official reason for her journey, she obtained an appointment to represent India at the Pacific Relations Conference then about to meet at Hot Springs, Virginia, under the auspices of the Council for World Affairs.

The Americans, long critical of the British attitude towards India, helped her so far as they could and gave her a visa, her only travel document. She had no money to pay for the journey, so an American officer, General Stratemeyer, whom she had met in Calcutta, offered her a seat on an Army transport plane, and friends in America made advance arrangements for her lectures through the Clark Getts Agency. With characteristic intrepidity she accepted the Army plane with its bucket seats and juvenile pilots, while Rita, aged fifteen, followed her by sea. The young girl, travelling alone from New York on her way to Hot Springs, proved as well able to answer journalistic enquiries as her older sisters.

'With someone in the family always in prison, it is rather hard to have a real home,' she told the Press. 'I am the only one in the family who hasn't been in prison yet, but I guess that's because I am too young.'

When Vijaya Lakshmi stepped off the transport plane in December 1944, she began a totally new life. When the war broke out a National

---

[1] The Chiang Kai-Sheks were then in America on a hush-hush mission to try to reconcile India and Britain, whose Allies they were. They wanted India on the side of the Allies against the Japanese, who were already in Burma.

E

# 66 *Envoy Extraordinary*

Committee for Indian Freedom had been formed in Washington, and a Muslim supporter of the national movement who had spent many years in America, Dr Syud Hossain, became its Chairman. At this time Britain was spending thousands of rupees from the Indian Treasury on pro-British propaganda, and well-known personalities, such as Beverley Nichols, came over to put Britain's case. The business of Dr Hossain's Committee now included the organization of platforms for Vijaya Lakshmi when she reached America to become the voice of independent India.

She found herself earning money for the first time, and appreciating the experience. The Clark Getts Agency presented her as 'one of the world's most important women of our time, notable for her great ideals and deep personal sacrifices for the benefit of her people'. 'Her strength,' added the folder advertisement with greater prophetic perspicacity than the writer can have realized, 'will be felt even more widely in the post-war years.' With jubilant optimism it went on to state that Mrs Pandit was an ardent advocate of Democracy who hoped to deliver the American Way of economic and political liberty . . . to her own 400 million people, 'and believes that the world will be benefited by these advances beyond our fondest present dreams.'

A list of her lecture topics followed:

'What Kind of Post-war World?'
'Four Freedoms for Asia'.
'Why India wants Independence'.
'Democratic Guarantees of Peace'.
'The Hope for World Betterment'.
'The Coming Indian Democracy'.

On one of these challenging subjects she spoke at the Independence Day meeting at Washington on January 29, 1945, and at the Book-Author Luncheon at the Hotel Astor on March 6th, where her fellow-speakers were Elizabeth Hawes, dress-designer and writer, and the war correspondent, Leland Stowe.

She was introduced by another well-known journalist, Irita Van Doren, Editor of the *Herald Tribune* Weekly Book Review, as 'one of the most notable women of our time'.

Of her Independence Day address the correspondent of the *Amrita Bazar Patrika* (Calcutta) reported on February 2nd: 'She spoke in fervent softness and not sensationally. Her voice was barely carried to the back of the room, so intense quiet prevailed most of the time in order to catch the words.' At the end Dr Hossain put the resolution:

## Courage in Herself 67

'This public meeting of the citizens of Washington calls on the United States Government to represent to the British Government who are our allies the desirability of immediate release of 10,000 political prisoners who have been imprisoned in India without any trial, and further to follow up this necessary preliminary to help achieve India's constitutional freedom now in accordance with the Atlantic Charter Principles. We believe such action is necessary for speedy victory in the Far East and achieving lasting peace.'

In the midst of these engagements, and of all the other demands which a lecture tour makes on the chief performer, she did not forget to wire roses to her daughters on the anniversary of Ranjit's death 'to keep his memory fragrant'. Roses and kindred extravagances were part of her reaction from the Puritan austerity imposed by Gandhi and the national movement upon those who led the struggle for independence.

During a radio address on January 28, 1945, she had struck the keynote for many subsequent discussions.

'India and America have been drawing closer together. 1942 was a year of problems in both countries when 80,000 of India's best people were detained in prison and famine took hold of the land through the negligence of government ...

'America at that period was passing too through crisis but she had won her freedom; she has the four freedoms. The Indian Congress stands for freedom; it has no quarrel with Englishmen; it is imperialism it opposes. Congress recognizes no distinctions of race, caste, creed or sex ... India presents a moral challenge; India's freedom will influence the peace and happiness of the whole world and the interdependence of the nations of the world.'

From New York she moved to Washington, where her challenging presence created problems not only for the British but for the American administration. According to the *Hindustan Standard* (Calcutta) for January 4, 1945, Mrs Roosevelt declared her inability to receive Mrs Pandit at the White House. Though British influence had clearly been at work, she added that she would gladly meet her outside it. Speaking at the Independence Day meeting on January 29th, Vijaya Lakshmi contributed a few significant facts.

'Literacy (in India) is 7 or 8 per cent though the British have been there 200 years. Literacy went up 100 per cent under Congress experiment. There is no medical aid in the country and nothing more is done for lack of funds. But salaries paid to Government officers are high.'

# 68 Envoy Extraordinary

Skilfully she added a story likely to arouse the emotions of listeners already critical of British behaviour.

'During an epidemic, a high British official was asked how many had died. He replied there was no epidemic; only two people had died. "What about the 7,000?" he was asked. "Oh, they were Indians. The two who died were Britishers," he replied.'

Vehemently she concluded: 'Imperialism, colonisation—those words stink . . . The world has to be made safe for everyone who lives in it, no matter the caste, creed, or colour of skin. We need the contribution of all the countries of the world to build up the type of world we want for our children and their children.'

The appreciative London audiences who only a decade later listened to her graceful speeches as Indian High Commissioner would never have guessed the quality of the passion once aroused by British complacency in the rebel who appeared in the United States as the embodiment of Asia's conscience and Asia's claims.

Ahead of her in April lay the San Francisco Conference, which had taken the place of the once expected Peace Conference in the official hope that an explosion of moral uplift would subdue, at any rate for the time being, the demands of countries preparing to confront the victorious Allies with a thorny selection of incompatible claims. All the Indian organizations in America were determined that Vijaya Lakshmi should appear in San Francisco at that crucial time. Though she had no official position they knew that she would have a superlative nuisance value, for she intended to insist that the official Indian delegation, handpicked by the British and led by Sir Ramaswami Mundaliar and Sir Firoz Khan Noon, did not represent the true India's point of view. The more difficult she made their task, the more successful her mission would be.[1]

The huge Assembly which opened on April 25th at the San Francisco Opera House subsequently became known to cynical journalists as the 'San Fiasco' Conference. One British correspondent emphasized the painful contrast between the 'stupendous opera' of the garishly lighted Californian stage and the 'bloody muddle' of Europe's concluding war. In three weeks many basic differences of opinion among the 'Big Three' (the United States, Britain and Russia) emerged from behind the roaring, rushing swirl of life at San Francisco, in which pressmen were 'milling round' from 8 a.m. until past midnight, and

---

[1] She has since explained that after Independence these distinguished pro-British collaborators were used by their country, which needed all the talent at its command, and were never treated as Quislings.

# Courage in Herself 69

experts attached to the delegations complained that they were given no time for meals.

On May 8th America's subdued celebration of VE Day owed something to the recent death of President Roosevelt, but the struggle with Japan had always bulked larger in American eyes than the war with Nazi Germany, and this view appeared in the headline with which the *New York Post* announced the end of the fighting in Europe: 'Now We Must Crush the Japs!' It was, of course, the Asian perspective which interested Vijaya Lakshmi, and her coming fight for India was to be exuberantly aided by the traditional American distrust of British diplomacy, which was suspected, not undeservedly, of seeking to restore the balance of power by playing off the United States and Russia against each other.

Vijaya Lakshmi left for San Francisco on April 17th after a lecture at Springfield, Ohio, in which she told her listeners at the Senior High School auditorium that she wished to help create an understanding between India and America 'because fundamentally our ideals and yours are much closer together than either are with the British.[1] I am a realist with my feet on the ground,' she added, 'and I want to keep them there. India is a country of poverty, ignorance, disease. I am interested in food and schools and medicine and freedom—those solid, practical things my people need.'

In San Francisco, where she stayed with Mrs Ogden Livingston Mills, the wife of a former Under-Secretary to the US Treasury, red and white posters advertising her meeting on April 27th appeared all over the city. She found the air brittle with a suppressed epidemic excitement, and the city brilliantly decorated with flags and flowers. The windows of the department stores had been arranged with special care, some showing fabrics patterned on international themes, and others concentrating on specific exhibits for the various countries represented.

Union Square displayed a sanguine glory of crimson rhododendrons, and the central St Francis Hotel was continuously mobbed with delegates and sightseers. Most of the recognizable celebrities kept off the streets, which nevertheless had plenty of exotic strollers to satisfy the curious—burnoused Arabs; Russian soldiers, tough and unamused; an occasional French general; gesticulating Latin-Americans; and a few unmistakable British officials protected by their determined air of reticent distinction.

---

[1] It seems possible that she may have modified this opinion after two years as Indian Ambassador to Washington (1949–51) and seven (1954–61) as Indian High Commissioner in Britain.

70         *Envoy Extraordinary*

It was generally understood that Vijaya Lakshmi's arrival in San Francisco caused some uneasiness to this final group, especially as at this time the National Committee for India's Freedom published, from its headquarters at the office of the India-China Trading Company, a large pamphlet called *The Voice of India*. To this publication some eminent Americans such as Pearl Buck, Louis Bromfield, and Congressmen Celler and Coffee had contributed articles supporting Indian independence.

Pearl Buck wrote prophetically: 'There is a fire and heat in India which cannot be cooled. India must be given its freedom or India will take its freedom . . . It is not entirely impossible that out of the Second World War a new India will be born, not quietly and with peace, but with storm and violence.'

Indian Nationalists who had followed Vijaya Lakshmi to California told the Press that they believed permission to leave India would have been withheld from her had she not been invited to the United States by Americans whom it would have been diplomatically difficult to refuse. They added that a recent visit to America by the Viceroy, Lord Wavell, seemed to them to have some connection with Mrs Pandit's lecture programme.

Officially she appeared in San Francisco to speak at two public meetings in the Scottish Rite Auditorium on April 27th and May 11th, sponsored by the National Committee for India's Freedom.

Advance Press notices announced jubilantly: 'One of the highlights of next month's United Nations world security conference will be the presence here of Mrs Vijaya Lakshmi Pandit, the beautiful, dark-eyed —and politically significant—sister of the imprisoned Nationalist leader, Jawaharlal Nehru.' And a highlight she certainly proved to be.

She began on April 20th with a packed Press Conference of 150 correspondents at the Mark Hopkins Hotel, overlooking the city and bay, where Anthony Eden and the official Indian delegation were staying. To the eagerly expectant journalists, she declared that these Indian delegates had not 'the slightest representative capacity, no sanction or mandate from any responsible groups in India', and were merely the nominees of the British Government. An elderly Hindu editor, Amritlal D. Sheth, newly arrived from Bombay, placed a huge garland of flowers round Vijaya Lakshmi's neck and crisply supplemented this charge. The Government of India Budget, he said, which included the salaries and expenses of the official delegation, had been rejected by the Central Legislature of India, but an attempt by the Assembly to debate

## Courage in Herself 71

whether or not the delegation represented India had been prevented by Viceregal veto.

From the audience an Indian Muslim, later discovered to be a guest at the hotel, heckled the speaker on 'Nationalist responsibility for undermining the Indian war effort'. Immediately the fierce Nehru temper flared up, followed by a display of pyrotechnics in which Vijaya Lakshmi demanded that he leave the room. Amid shouts from Indians in the audience: 'He's a British propagandist agent!' the interrupter hurriedly departed. She went on to underline her theme as a spokesman not only for India but for all Asia.

'Beside the 400 millions of the people of India there are another 200 million subject peoples in Asia who have been under various European imperialistic powers and are now under the subjugation of Japan, who are looking to the freedom of India as the assurance of their own freedom. India is the pivot of the whole system of imperialism and colonialism which always breeds war. India's freedom, therefore, is an acid test of the principle for which this war has been fought, and the continued denial of Indian freedom by Britain is a negation of those principles and of the sacrifices that have been made to win victory.'

Thenceforward she packed San Francisco's largest halls wherever she appeared. Reporters abandoned the respectable proceedings of the official Indian delegation as soon as she, the inspired avenger of her husband and father, held a Press Conference herself, though they found it difficult to keep up with her physically. Directly she learned that Lord Halifax, the British Ambassador, had delivered a speech to the Californian State Legislature at Sacramento, she sped to the famous city among the gold-rush mountains where her coming was awaited with enthusiasm.

A large enough number of Indians had settled in the Sacramento Valley, where palm trees marking the horizon brought nostalgic memories of their native land, to constitute a little India within the United States. Most of these Indians were farmers, of whom some had come a distance of 200 miles to hear Mrs Pandit. Some of them owned fruit orchards and others leased thousands of acres to grow rice. Though the majority were Sikhs, all but a few had given up their turbans and beards.

A rousing reception greeted Vijaya Lakshmi when she arrived at noon, to be officially received by the Mayor, the Commissioner of Police, and 400 Indians from every part of the State. Put into a car bedecked by the American flag and the Tricolour of the Indian National

# Envoy Extraordinary

Congress, she was piloted by police motor cycles and taken in procession to the hotel where another 200 Indians awaited her. The Secretary of the Bharat Welfare League, Nanalal Patel, commented afterwards: 'Never in the history of the Indian community in San Joaquin Valley has such a demonstration taken place.'

At the meeting, where Dr Hossain as usual presided, she repeated her theme-song to an enraptured body of local legislators.

'All subject races must be liberated. The independence of all colonial peoples is a vital concern of freedom-loving peoples everywhere.'

When the war in Europe was over and the United Nations tentatively established, she left San Francisco for an apartment in New York found by her daughters. She did not much like this temporary residence, and eventually discovered another close to a liquor shop in a peculiar location off Park Avenue. But it was their largest apartment up to date, with two bedrooms, a living-room and a dining-room.

Nayantara has recorded her pleasant impression of the cheerfully-lit living-room above the liquor store, and its dancing fire. She also remarked that in the midst of their studies and personal problems, the two girls had hardly noticed their mother's 'singular growth in stature', during her year in America without Ranjit's affectionate support.

They were still in the first apartment when the news came through, in late July, of England's General Election and the Labour victory. To begin with the event did not mean very much to them; other Labour Governments had gone to Westminster with little subsequent effect on Britain's policy towards India, and few Indians could have been expected to realize the constitutional distinction between office and power. Though Indian independence had been a plank in the Labour platform and two future Ministers, F. W. Pethick-Lawrence and Sir Stafford Cripps, had included the demand for it in their election addresses, it was not until the Cabinet Mission of 1946 in which they both took part that India became convinced of Britain's sincere desire to set her free.[1] Twelve months went by before Indians began to appreciate the fundamental difference between the British Raj in India and the new Government in Socialist Britain.

The first clear indication of future changes came on a hot summer day when Vijaya Lakshmi and her daughters learned that Jawaharlal Nehru had been set free after 1,042 days of close confinement, 960 in

---

[1] No little credit must go to Sir Stafford and his Bristol constituency for the rôle they played in this crusade by constituency resolution to the Labour Party Conference, in which they received support from other constituency parties and were seconded by the Chelsea party, of which Professor George Catlin was then the Chairman.

## Courage in Herself 73

Ahmednagar Fort and the remainder at the notorious Bareilly, with a day in Naini Prison *en route*. He was released from the District Jail in Almora, the beautiful and remote hill station among the foothills of the Himalayas close to the Pandits' country home, and his first action was to visit Khali as a token of respect and affection for his lost brother-in-law.

Vijaya Lakshmi decided to remain in America until the spring, for her time until Christmas was solidly booked with lectures in the South and Middle West, and after a January tour of the East she had promised to return to the Pacific Coast. But in September the Viceroy, Lord Wavell, announced that a Constituent Assembly would be summoned as soon as elections, which had not taken place since 1937, could be arranged. To begin with the Indian leaders felt no confidence in their reality but eventually the elections were held, for the Central Legislative Assembly in December 1945 and the Provincial Legislatures in the spring of 1946.

The elections to the Central Assembly showed an overwhelming success for Congress, with 91 per cent of the votes in the general constituencies, while every Muslin constituency was won by Mr Jinnah's organization, the Muslim League. These crucial pointers to the future meant that Vijaya Lakshmi could remain in America no longer; she must return to take up her Portfolio in the United Provinces and await the coming election.

At the end of January 1946, she returned to India, the only woman passenger on the US Army's air transport command air-liner which travelled by way of Bermuda, Casablanca and Cairo to Karachi. At the airport to see her off were Dr Syud Hossain, Dr Anup Singh, the Secretary of the National Committee for India's Freedom, and the Indian correspondent and author, Dr Krishnalal Shridharani. In March Lekha followed her to India; the other two girls remained at College in the United States until 1947.

CHAPTER 6

# Crusader into Ambassador

AT first India's Nationalists had welcomed the British Labour victory, and Maulana Azad, then President of Congress, sent a telegram of congratulation to the new Prime Minister, Clement Attlee. The appointment of Lord Pethick-Lawrence as Secretary of State for India was also a welcome change from that of his predecessor, Leo Amery, though India hoped soon to see this office, symbolic of its subjection, abolished altogether. But the Congress leaders and the Muslim League had alike felt uneasy about the suggested elections, which seemed yet another British device for creating delay.

The well-intentioned Labour Government found its sincere aspirations for Indian independence doubted and criticized. Lord Pethick-Lawrence, in his essay on Gandhi, subsequently recorded the questionable welcome which awaited their policy: 'In face of our determination to emancipate India from British rule, we were confronted with political deadlock. Gandhi had lost faith in British intentions about Indian freedom, Jinnah had lost faith in fair treatment for Muslims at the hands of a Hindu majority.'

Vijaya Lakshmi returned to India to find this mood of uneasy suspicion, but the atmosphere was none the less totally changed from that which had surrounded her departure in December 1944. There were at least no restrictions to hinder family reunions. Her brother had attended the abortive Simla Conference of June 1945, arranged by the Conservative (Caretaker) British Government carrying on between the end of the European war and the General Election in the belief that it had at least another year of office, and hoping to find a co-operative Indian Government with which to finish the war against Japan. Jawaharlal had played no special part in this typical contest between Congress and the Muslim League, and when it was over he went for a long-postponed holiday in Kashmir in order to reinvigorate his jaded senses with the loveliness of the snow-crowned peaks and the vivid blue-greens of river and valley and lake.

## Crusader into Ambassador 75

He wrote later in *The Unity of India*: 'I wandered about like one possessed and drunk with beauty, and the intoxication of it filled my mind.'

To allay Indian anxiety and bitterness, the British Government sent out a Parliamentary delegation representative of all parties which was already travelling round India when Vijaya Lakshmi arrived. As its conscientious endeavours had little effect upon the prevailing sense of frustration, the Viceroy assured the newly-elected Legislative Assembly that the British Government was determined to bring an Indian constitution-making body into being as soon as possible, and on February 19, 1946, the Prime Minister in the British House of Commons announced the forthcoming departure to India of a special Cabinet Mission. Its purpose was to smooth the path towards Independence, and its three members would be the Secretary of State, Lord Pethick-Lawrence; Sir Stafford Cripps, President of the Board of Trade; and Mr (later Earl) A. V. Alexander, the First Lord of the Admiralty.

The elections to the Central Legislative Assembly, held in December 1945, had made evident the political division of India between two great parties. The same tendency revealed itself in the provincial elections of the early spring. Congress formed provincial ministries in eight of the eleven Provinces, and one of these took office in the United Provinces where the Ministers had all resigned on the outbreak of war.

To add to the turmoil in the country the trial of members of the Indian National Army led by Subhas Bose occurred during that winter, while minor mutinies in RAF stations in India, ending in a major explosion during February in Bombay, symbolized the declining authority of the British Raj.

Now that the former Ministry was re-established, Vijaya Lakshmi returned to Lucknow to take charge of her Portfolio as Minister of Local Government and Public Health, and was subsequently elected to the Constituent Assembly convened, with her brother as President, in December 1946 five months after the Cabinet Mission had left the scene of its uneasy labours.

Here too the results were wholly decisive, with Congress holding 205 of the 296 seats allotted to British India.[1] Jawaharlal's position had been established after a Presidential election in which Gandhi's influence had caused him to prevail over the two other candidates, Sardar Patel and Acharya Kripalani (then Congress General Secretary). Almost

---

[1] The Princes had not yet joined the discussions, and the Muslim League, represented at the first meeting of the Assembly on December 9th by empty chairs, had refused to attend.

# 76 Envoy Extraordinary

immediately he had to face the beginning of communal civil war, precipitated by the Muslim League's Direct Action Day on August 16th. This mutual massacre was subsequently known as 'the Great Calcutta Killing', in which Hindu-Muslim ferocity caused 5,000 deaths and 15,000 injuries in four terrible days. Prolonged tragedy overshadowed the deliberations of Jawaharlal's Interim Government, which would otherwise have been brilliantly invigorated by the prospect of Independence at last on the horizon.

Vijaya Lakshmi's own career now took the decisive turning which was to determine its direction for the next fifteen years. Her spectacular performance at San Francisco meant that international diplomacy rather than national politics was to demand her talents, and in October 1946 she left the turbulent Indian scene for her first official mission outside her own country.

It was the Viceroy, Lord Wavell—doubtless influenced by the inconveniences for himself and his Government of her self-appointed rôle at San Francisco—who insisted that Mrs Pandit should lead the Indian delegation to the second part of the opening session of the United Nations Assembly in New York and thus become the first woman to head such a mission.[1] When Lord Wavell recommended her Jawaharlal had been hesitant, and Gandhi warned her that she should expect the worst. Only a few lip-service votes, he thought, would come her way, for the Indian delegation had a difficult and delicate task to perform. Its chief function was to denounce the apartheid policies of the South African Government, and especially to publicize that Government's treatment of South Africa's Indian minority, which had a long history.

This Indian colony had developed from the indentured labour brought to South Africa in 1860 to sustain the Natal sugar industry. Established there for the white man's convenience, the Indians had proved to be good traders and useful citizens; they had started many small businesses in isolated communities which helped to supply local populations cut off from large towns, and thus created a modest prosperity for the villages where they settled. To bring a measure of political organization to this growing colony, Gandhi had gone to South Africa in 1897 and remained till 1914. In 1904 he established a settlement at Phoenix in Natal, which was in effect his first ashram, and founded the journal *Indian Opinion*. When he returned to India he left his second son Manilal to carry on his work and edit the magazine. The settlement

---

[1] The first part had opened in London on January 10, 1946. In April the League of Nations had closed its work and had given its physical assets to the United Nations.

# Crusader into Ambassador 77

continued until Manilal's death in April 1956. A year or two later it had to close, and the paper ceased publication.

From the establishment of the Union Government in 1910 restrictions had been imposed on the Indian minority, and Gandhi started his non-violent resistance movement in South Africa—for which he studied the technique of Britain's Suffragettes—in protest against this injustice. The Liberal Viceroy, Lord Hardinge, who succeeded Lord Minto in 1911, publicly supported Gandhi's campaign against South Africa's 'invidious and unjust laws'. The Viceroy's candour alarmed the Government in London, but his uncompromising words brought the unanimous support of India for Britain in the First World War.

Racial tension nevertheless continued, and the unfair discrimination against Indians was part of it. When Winifred Holtby, as a young writer in her twenties, visited South Africa in 1926, she wrote home from Johannesburg:

'South Africa probably is on the eve of a big crisis but it will be a colour crisis ... The next twenty years must see some big changes here. The stupidity and selfishness of the average South African in the face of the colour danger is amazing—and the danger only arises because of that selfish stupidity.'[1]

In 1946 the twenty years referred to by Winifred Holtby had passed and the changes had come but not for the better, though Field-Marshal Smuts, Prime Minister at the time of Winifred's visit, was still the dominant figure in South African politics.

The second part of the First Session of the United Nations Assembly opened on October 23, 1946, at Flushing Meadows, New York, under the Presidency of Mr P.-H. Spaak of Belgium, with Vice-Presidents representing China, France, South Africa, the USSR, the United Kingdom, the United States, and Venezuela. The atmosphere of optimism, as in the earlier meetings, recalled the beginning of the League of Nations at Geneva in 1920, but the new organization had more experience behind it. Once again a great experiment in human relationships was being launched. Surely it would avoid the disastrous mistakes which had wrecked its predecessor? Surely the much-tested leaders of nations which had passed through apocalyptic experiences twice in thirty years had learned enough to achieve peace through mutual understanding?

As described by Nayantara, who was present with Rita, the room in

[1] *Selected Letters of Winifred Holtby and Vera Brittain* (March 15, 1926), London and Hull (A. Brown) 1960.

# 78 Envoy Extraordinary

which the opening discussions began was both beautiful and comfortable. A giant map of the world on a wall behind the dais showed that international leadership no longer lay exclusively with three or four prominent Western nations; the East was also beginning to play its part. For the first time India was represented at an international Conference by delegates whom her own Government, though not yet fully independent, had selected. Celebrities, as at San Francisco, turned up in every corridor; they included Britain's Ernest Bevin, solid, blunt, and shrewd, and his *bête noir* Andrei Vishinsky, whose blue eyes could sparkle with gaiety or harden with hatred. The Emir Feisal of Saudi Arabia, in flowing colourful robes, provided a glamorous contrast with Denmark's sedate woman delegate, later the Danish Minister to Iceland.

India's case against South Africa was a protest, in particular, against the Asiatic Land Tenure Act and the Indian Representation Act, which denied full human rights to South Africa's Indian residents, and impaired friendly relations between India and South Africa. India requested the General Assembly to advise South Africa to reconsider and revise these measures. She had, it appeared, the support of most of the nations present.

This question was to be debated in the Joint Committee, a combined session of the Political and Security, and the Legal Committees. The Chairman had suggested that a sub-committee might examine the issue, but the Ukrainian delegate, Mr Dmitro Z. Manuilsky, who was Chairman of the Political and Security Committee, protested that the question was too vital to be relegated to a sub-committee. In the debate that followed the Polish delegate remarked that South Africa's behaviour to Indians recalled the Nazis' treatment of the Poles, and the Chinese delegate said that the Asiatic Land Tenure Act discriminated against all Asians.

Field-Marshal Smuts, South Africa's Prime Minister and a great international figure, made a restrained speech on behalf of his country, and Vijaya Lakshmi did the same for hers. Controversy began when another South African delegate, Mr Heaton Nicholls, accused India of treating her own Untouchables worse than his country treated Indians. This seemed a curious argument for retaining the *status quo*. He went on to say that South Africa maintained Christian civilization 'in a dark continent inhabited by primitive natives and polygamous races'.

'I am not aware,' commented Vijaya Lakshmi to the delight of the non-European delegations, 'that polygamy, whether sanctioned by law or not, is limited to the East.' She added that if Christ Himself visited South Africa, he would be treated as a 'prohibited immigrant'.

## Crusader into Ambassador 79

The final voting on the debate took place on December 7th at a tense late session which continued until 2 a.m. It resulted in an historic resolution being adopted 'on the Report of the Joint First and Sixth Committees', by the necessary two-thirds majority:

'The General Assembly,

Having taken note of the application made by the Government of India regarding the treatment of Indians in the Union of South Africa, and having considered the matter:

(1) States that, because of that treatment, friendly relations between the two Member States have been impaired and, unless a satisfactory settlement is reached, these relations are likely to be further impaired;

(2) Is of the opinion that the treatment of Indians in the Union should be in conformity with the international obligations under the agreements concluded between the two Governments and the relevant provisions of the Charter;

(3) Therefore requests the two Governments to report at the next Session of the General Assembly the means adopted to this effect.'[1]

Vijaya Lakshmi's friends and daughters rushed up to her table to congratulate her, but her sense of victory was impaired by a remark which Field-Marshal Smuts had made after her first impressive speech. Nayantara records that her mother then went up to him and quietly mentioned a significant injunction laid on her in India.

'I hope I have not said anything of a personal nature to hurt you. My instructions from Gandhiji before I left home were that I should shake your hand and ask your blessing for my case.'

The ageing Prime Minister, perhaps foreseeing the political defeat which he was to encounter two years later, answered ruefully: 'My child, you may win, but this will be a hollow victory for you.'

He spoke truly, for the victory was purely verbal. After the defeat of the Smuts' Government in 1948, the three Nationalist Prime Ministers who followed him, Doctors Malan, Strydom, and Verwoerd, each carried to a further extreme the policy now known as *apartheid*. This policy burdened the Indian community almost more than the African, since its members were regarded as foreigners in South Africa though some Indian families had been established there for three generations. By 1960 nearly half a million Indians were living in the Union, of

---

[1] Fifty-second plenary meeting, December 8, 1946. One Indian journalist (Iqbal Singh in the *Illustrated Weekly* of India) described the passage of this Resolution, despite every device of evasion and obfuscation by some 'great' powers, as Mrs Pandit's 'finest hour'.

# 80                    *Envoy Extraordinary*

whom about 350,000 were resident in Natal. Under the complicated Group Areas Act of 1950 (with additions in 1957) the Africans were deprived of the small proportion of land—about 8 per cent of the total area—which they had been able to buy in such places as Sophiatown, but the Indians fared even worse. Many were dispossessed of thriving businesses, and all were scheduled for gradual removal to suburban areas where they must start again from scratch. The South African Government regarded them as wholly without rights; the underlying purpose of the persecutions they had to suffer was to compel them, through the pressure of imposed poverty, to seek repatriation in an India where they had never lived.[1]

In 1963, when Vijaya Lakshmi again led an Indian delegation to the United Nations a decade after being President of the Assembly, she spoke to a New York Press Conference of the South African issue which had been before the Assembly for seventeen years. The sadly prophetic comment of Field-Marshal Smuts echoed through her words when she said: 'Every time while the Assembly passed resolutions the situation in South Africa was deteriorating further'. Yet her speech at the time of her resounding triumph at the first Assembly, which sent her name echoing round the world, remained true in principle, and few nations would today reject it.

'I ask no favour for India . . . no concession for the Indian population of South Africa. I ask for the verdict of this Assembly on a proven violation of the Charter; on an issue which has led to acute dispute between two member states; on an issue which is not confined to India or South Africa; and finally on an issue the decision of which must make or mar the loyalty and confidence which the common people of the world have placed on us. Mine is an appeal to a conscience, the conscience of the world which this Assembly is.'

When Vijaya Lakshmi left New York in December 1946, the United Press reported her belief that she had been 'shadowed' during her stay there, and added that the British strongly disapproved of her association with the Russian delegates—an association which was to bear diplomatic fruit immediately after Independence. To a journalist on

---

[1] When I was entertained on July 17, 1960, by an Indian Group at the Oriental Club ten miles from Durban, I learned that many of the city's 205,000 Indians were to suffer this fate. One area with 40,000 Indians had been proclaimed white, so that the Indian owners of property could not develop or extend it. Those living in this district were shortly to be moved to a hilly terrain outside Durban. The idea of the Government, said the speaker, was to reserve the whole Durban area for the white population.

V.B.

## Crusader into Ambassador 81

*The People's Voice* she praised the Russian representatives, and said: 'When I thanked the leader of the Russian delegation for support in the case against South Africa, he said he would not accept my thanks because he had voted for justice and not for India.'

Before she went home she received a sincere tribute from an American poet, Edith Lovejoy Pierce, which moved her greatly:

> Frail figurehead on the long galleon's prow,
> Sheer from your woman's grace the wide ship flares,
> Fans out behind the apex of your brow.
> Your native India as a banner wears
> Your front of freedom. The oppressed in lands
> Far off their full grey tedium break,
> Turn like a restless wave stirred by your hands,
> Follow as foam in the white watery wake.
>
> Now a tall rock blots out the noonday sun,
> Covers the light of your calm universe,
> Forces your ship in shadow world to run,
> Casts on the sea a dark and angular curse.
> But all the elements are on your side:
> Lightly you walk on water, step on sea.
> The slow processional of the deep tide
> Bears you beyond the dreaded island's lee—
> Bears you to light, but grinds the barren stone,
> Claws the imperial rock down to a skeleton bone.

The India to which Vijaya Lakshmi returned as a Congress Minister had already entered the period in which eminent Indians would no longer be shadowed by British agents. The birth-throes that preceded Independence had now become painfully conspicuous in a series of accelerating events. In June 1946 the British Cabinet Mission had gone home, compelled to leave its task only half fulfilled; on September 2nd the Interim Government headed by Jawaharlal Nehru—nominally the Viceroy's Executive Council, but widely described as 'The Cabinet'— had taken office and held a first meeting, in which empty chairs symbolized the non-co-operation of the Muslim League.

Early in 1947 the British Government had confronted the Hindu-Muslim deadlock by announcing its intention to transfer power 'into responsible Indian hands not later than June 1948'. During March a new and dynamic Viceroy, Lord Mountbatten, had succeeded Lord Wavell, and within three months had decided that, against a background of increasing communal riots, even 1948 would be too late.

F

# 82        *Envoy Extraordinary*

In consultation with him, the British Government fixed August 15, 1947, as the date on which it would in fact quit India. On that day two new Dominions came into being, to be immediately involved in communal strife, which lasted for sixteen months and caused an estimated total death-roll of half a million persons.[1]

These fearful events were already in progress when Nayantara Sahgal returned in October from the United States, to find a transformed India in which her uncle, whom she had left as a prisoner, was the Prime Minister, and their old friend Sarojini Naidu, who had wept over the humiliation of Indians after Amritsar, had become the Governor of the United Provinces. The only home that Tara had known, Anand Bhawan, was a locked and empty shell, the mournful abode of ghosts who had played their part in the creation of an independent India, but had now transferred their tasks into the hands of those who would mould their country's destiny.

Her mother too had gone, for Vijaya Lakshmi had her own special task in the creation of that future. Shortly after the transfer of power she had joined India's new Foreign Service, and had been appointed to establish the Indian Embassy in Moscow as its first Ambassador.

---

[1] In his book *Pakistan* (Ernest Benn, 1963) Mr Ian Stephens compares this appalling figure with the military death-roll (officially given in round figures as 540,000) of the entire British Commonwealth, including civilians killed in air raids, during the six years of the Second World War.

CHAPTER 7

# Soviet Citadel

WHEN independent India entered the field of international diplomacy, she had three major objectives of comparable importance. The first was to bring the ideals of Mahatma Gandhi into the political world and give them practical reality; the second meant establishing India as a great democracy in a continent where communism was rampant; the third involved making the economic poverty of India real to the world community of nations, and as far as possible arranging for some of her urgent needs to be met by countries with superabundant resources. When Independence came, the average income of her people was no more than $50 per person per year, or less than one dollar a week.[1]

From the first objective came the policy of non-alignment, so often defined by Jawaharlal Nehru in his speeches on foreign affairs. 'We propose,' he said in the Constituent Assembly on December 4, 1947, 'to keep on the closest terms of friendship with other countries unless they themselves create difficulties. We shall be friends with America . . . We intend co-operating with the Soviet Union.'

Ten years later, in a debate on Foreign Affairs in the Lok Sabha (the People's or Lower House in Parliament) on December 9, 1958, he was able to describe more clearly the principles behind this policy.

'When we say our policy is one of non-alignment, obviously we mean non-alignment with military blocs. It is not a negative policy. It is a positive one, a definite one and, I hope, a dynamic one. But, in so far as the military blocs today and the cold war are concerned, we do not align ourselves with either bloc. This in itself is not a policy; it is only part of a policy . . . The policy itself can only be a policy of acting according to our best judgment, and furthering the principal objectives and ideals that we have . . . We realize that our influence in such matters can only be limited, because we are not in possession of, nor have we

---

[1] B. K. Nehru, Ambassador of India to the United States of America: *Speaking of India* (p. 15). Information Service of India, Washington 8, D.C. 1964.

# 84 Envoy Extraordinary

the capacity to possess, weapons like the modern nuclear weapons. Still our influence has not been negligible. This is not because we ourselves are influential, but because we do believe that what we have said in regard to peace has found an echo in people's hearts and minds in all countries ... The other positive aspects are an enlargement of freedom in the world, replacement of colonialism by free and independent countries, and a larger degree of co-operation among nations.'

One practical interpretation of this policy, as Vijaya Lakshmi so often explained in her later speeches in the United States, at the United Nations, and in Britain, meant that India would endeavour to act as a 'bridge' between nations with differing ideals, and in general to play the part of 'honest broker' and peacemaker in the quarrels of other states. Too often the verbal expression of this noble and urgently-needed intention had a self-righteous sound which irritated the more cynical diplomats of long-established nations. A former member of the State Department once told the author of this book that Indian officials in Washington tended to make themselves unpopular by too many didactic pronouncements about other people's conduct, while in Britain the more 'realistic' politicians permitted themselves almost a whoop of triumph when India took possession of Goa and later built up her defences against China in the old-fashioned manner, accepting help from countries to which Gandhi's ideals had seemed a fakir's phantasy.

The fact remains that India's difficult attempt to bring morality into politics represents one of the most crucial needs of the modern world, which will ultimately perish if Gandhi's vision of a non-violent society is destined to remain forever unfulfilled. It was once well said by a distinguished political scientist that in this world we have to be self-righteous before we can be righteous, and India's diplomats, like her first Prime Minister, have shown courage and determination in maintaining their standards notwithstanding critical disparagement from less dedicated colleagues, and in spite of their own failure to live up to them when faced with overwhelming international misfortune.

The endeavour to establish India as a great Asian democracy—numerically the largest democracy in the world—has been more conspicuously successful in spite of the difficulty of making such a conception real to a still largely illiterate population of 438 millions (one-seventh of mankind), of whom many still live at a subhuman level. In her three General Elections of 1952, 1957, and 1962, India has proved immensely resourceful in overcoming the difficulties of illiteracy

## Soviet Citadel 85

by the use of pictorial symbols, and remarkably successful in creating mass enthusiasm among nearly 200 million registered voters of whom 62 per cent exercised their right to vote in 1952 and 1957.[1]

Nevertheless, as Mr Nehru and his successors have repeatedly emphasized, the realities of foreign policy and the significance of democracy cannot become of fundamental importance to a huge population which is hungry, underclad, and inadequately housed. It is upon this problem that the fate of Indian democracy will probably turn. In the first two objects of her diplomatic missions, India has been able to appear as a leader (if not always successful) of other great peoples. But in putting forward the massive needs of a poverty-stricken nation she appears inevitably as a supplicant. Her chief difficulty has been to maintain the dignity established by the first two points of her triangular policy in a diplomatic world where 'face' (especially important to an oriental country) occupies a disproportionate rôle. Nothing has illustrated this problem more clearly than the tortuous negotiations over the Wheat Loan Agreement, which concerned India and the United States between 1949 and 1951 when Mrs Pandit was India's Ambassador to Washington.[2]

In Moscow none of these major objectives became real to Vijaya Lakshmi; they remained matters of profound but unattainable idealism. Stalin's Russia did not even begin to understand, much less appreciate, the ideals of Mahatma Gandhi, and the Communist Soviet State could hardly have been expected to value the democratic intentions of an India which—as her Prime Minister was to explain in a Foreign Affairs debate on December 10, 1950—did not propose to pursue a 'tender policy . . . in regard to communist activities'. Nor could the Soviet Union, as a 'have-not' power itself, be called upon to meet even the most modest of India's needs.

On April 14, 1947, the *Daily Telegraph* Special Correspondent in New Delhi had reported the first official announcement of India's decision to send an Ambassador to Moscow. 'Being desirous for maintaining and strengthening the friendly relations between India and Soviet Russia, the two Governments have decided to exchange diplomatic missions at Embassy level.'

After mentioning Vijaya Lakshmi as the probable choice, the Correspondent continued: 'Mrs Pandit led the Indian delegation to the United Nations last year. She attracted notice by her vigorous advocacy

---

[1] In the American Presidential election of 1956, the proportion of actual votes from 103 million potential voters was 61 per cent—or one per cent *less* than that of India.

[2] See Chapter 8.

# 86 Envoy Extraordinary

of the rights of Indians in South Africa. M. Molotov then said he would welcome her appointment in Russia.'

This Moscow assignment typified the intention of the prospective Indian Government, still four months from official existence, to establish embassies and legations in foreign countries which would operate, it was hoped, as so many goodwill missions.

'The impression we have been trying to give,' Vijaya Lakshmi said later in Moscow,[1] 'is that there is no question of antagonism against anybody, but we must have a period in which we can build up our own country economically—let the outside world judge us then . . . As for foreign policy, there is no reason why we should align ourselves with anybody. Certainly, the West has not made such a good job of it in the past, nor are its prospects for the future so very bright. We have our own independent foreign policy, and we have our own way of life —though we are willing to adapt certain good features whether in Russia or in the West.'

In December 1946, at a Press Conference in Delhi, held shortly after his sister's triumph at Flushing Meadows, Jawaharlal Nehru had been asked whether India intended sending other representative women to international conferences, as they had sent Mrs Pandit to the United Nations. He replied: 'We will be very glad to send them not only to these international conferences, but to appoint them permanently as ministers and ambassadors.'

Nevertheless, her appointment did not go through easily. In his long biography of Mr Nehru, Michael Brecher records of the period immediately preceding Independence:

'The slightest incident seemed capable of upsetting the precarious equilibrium created by the Mountbatten Plan. Less than a week after the Plan was informally approved by the leaders, a crisis arose in the Interim Government, one of many that bedevilled its fortunes. The issue was rather trivial, the proposed appointment of an Ambassador to Moscow. Liaquat Ali was vehemently opposed: Nehru insisted. To complicate matters the nominee was Mrs Pandit, Nehru's sister. The Viceroy succeeded in deferring the decision.[2]

No doubt the proposal to appoint Vijaya Lakshmi caused the type of basically irrelevant criticism which occurs when one family has several gifted members, as though the accident of relationship somehow impairs an individual's proven ability to do a job. Her brother

[1] *Manchester Guardian*, May 25, 1948.
[2] Michael Brecher, op. cit., p. 349.

## Soviet Citadel 87

had also defied convention not only by appointing a woman ambassador, but by giving her the toughest diplomatic spot on earth as the scene of her labours. The postponed decision allowed the claim of qualifications to prevail over petulant charges of nepotism combined with political objections to having an Indian Ambassador in Moscow at all, for when Vijaya Lakshmi visited Bombay in the last week of August 1947, she was the ambassador-designate about to leave for her formidable appointment.

Nevertheless there is not even one mention of her name in the Index to *India's Foreign Policy*, the huge volume of Mr Nehru's published speeches made between September 1946 and April 1961.[1] The nearest he ever came to a direct reference to her occurred in his speech on Non-Alignment (December 4, 1947), when he was discussing the previous session of the United Nations General Assembly: 'I should like to pay a tribute to our delegation, especially to the leader of the delegation.'

At a party given in Bombay by the Prime Minister, Mr B. G. Kher, subsequently an Indian High Commissioner in Britain, she referred to her new appointment in reply to his address of welcome, and said that many people had asked her whether she would not 'get lost' in the vast Soviet wilderness where she would be unfamiliar not only with the Russian language but with the customs of the people.

The Correspondent of *The Hindustani Times* quoted her response.

'Her reply to these fears was that she was fully conscious of what she had agreed to undertake. She did not minimize the importance of the task nor its delicacy and its gravity. She might have chosen England or America where she has contacts, where she is known, and with whose customs and language she is familiar. It would have been easier; settling down would have been no hard job as it was going to be in Russia. But that was precisely why she had chosen to go to Russia. She wanted to accept the challenge that Russia threw out.'

On August 5th she began her journey by flying over the snow-covered mountains between Basrah and Teheran. In Moscow a life-size painting of Stalin confronted her at the airport. Nine days later she presented her credentials as India's first Ambassador to the Soviet Union to Nikolai Shivernik, Chairman of the Presidium of the Supreme Soviet, where to her astonishment the efficient Russian interpreter addressed her in faultless Urdu. Early in September she quietly made a

[1] The Publications Division, Ministry of Information and Broadcasting, Government of India, p.p. 612, August 15, 1961.

# 88 Envoy Extraordinary

brief flight to Stockholm with Lekha, who had accompanied her to Moscow, in order to buy furniture and fittings for the new Embassy. This was temporarily a small, double-storeyed dwelling in a lane off a main road, but the Mission subsequently moved to a finely proportioned house which had once belonged to Serge Kuisevitsky, the conductor. With her usual skill Vijaya Lakshmi soon made it into a home for her officers and staff, especially after Tara joined her, bringing two Indian bearers whom the new Ambassador thankfully welcomed after the over-robust Russian maids.

She had hardly succeeded in equipping the Embassy when she had to leave for New York for the meeting of the United Nations Assembly again held at Flushing Meadows Park, which had been the scene of the World's Fair. During this second assignment as leader of the Indian delegation, the New York Press described her as 'a head-liner again'. Commenting that South Africa was once more her chief target, the Correspondent added that 'South Africa is sending a new and younger set of jousters to contend this year with the charm and oratory of Mrs Pandit'. But an even more formidable duel was impending between Eleanor Roosevelt and Andrei Vishinsky over the refusal, for political reasons, of Europe's displaced persons to return to their country of origin. Around the Conference table these two national leaders attacked each other uncompromisingly, though outside the Assembly their relationship was cordial and mutually respectful.

Vijaya Lakshmi reviewed in Delhi the work of the Indian delegation at this Assembly after her brief return to India in December. She regretted, she said, that the delegates sometimes allowed their better judgment to be over-ruled by temporary considerations of expediency; this had been particularly true with regard to the fight for the rights of Indians in South Africa. In consequence India's resolution on the subject had suffered a technical defeat, since it had polled nearly but not quite the necessary two-thirds of the votes cast.

'It is for the nations who voted against us or who abstained from voting,' she added, 'to reflect on the consequences of their action . . . I am glad to say that in spite of the difficult conditions which prevailed we adhered unswervingly to the principles of the Charter and successfully maintained the standards of independence and integrity that the world has come to expect of India.'

Vijaya Lakshmi visited the United Nations once more, in 1948, during her period as Ambassador to Moscow. After her appointment as Ambassador to Washington in March 1949 she ceased to lead the Indian delegation, though occasionally she appeared at the United

## Soviet Citadel 89

Nations to raise a special topic. When she was asked some years later how she managed to combine her rôle at the United Nations with her position as Ambassador to the Soviet Union in 1947 and 1948, she replied frankly that this had not been difficult.

'There was not much work in Moscow, and my Counsellor took charge during the time I was at the UN.'

Those two years indeed provided little instruction for the Embassy staff in the first-hand knowledge of diplomacy which all its members, from their leader downwards, had now to learn by experience. Vijaya Lakshmi's period as Ambassador covered the grimmest days of the iron régime of Joseph Stalin, who had become Soviet Premier in 1941 and remained in implacable control until his death in March 1953, four years after her departure from Moscow.

Even the warmth of her personality did not melt the Russian ice. She had gone to Moscow 'starry-eyed', as she confessed to a friend years later, for it was her first diplomatic appointment, and the Russians had been the Indians' only friends at the United Nations in 1945–46. But she soon discovered that even she had to share the limitations imposed on other envoys. No foreigner was allowed to go more than 55 kilometres from Moscow; occasionally she encountered trouble because she unwittingly went outside these prescribed limits. Much as she wanted to see Soviet Asia, Leningrad was the only city beyond Moscow that she managed to visit throughout her period as Ambassador.

She went there to inspect the 130-year-old University in July 1948, toured its extensive library, and saw Russian editions of such famous Indian classics as the *Ramayana* and the *Maha Bharata*. During her four days' stay she also inspected a local Buddhist temple and a mosque, and at a special new museum was shown hundreds of exhibits which told in detail the story of Leningrad's defence during the German invasion. According to the Moscow Press she exclaimed: 'No wonder the Russian Revolution took birth in this city!'

Vijaya Lakshmi never met Stalin, who was rumoured to be suffering from cancer; the first foreign Ambassador to be received by him was the American envoy, whom he saw during the war. She did however meet Molotov, Mikoyan and Khrushchev as junior politicians, and came to know Molotov better at the United Nations. He regarded her as a 'fiery girl', and at San Francisco had said that the voice of Free India was outside the Conference hall. In July 1957, eight years after she had left Moscow, he was ousted from the Communist Party and government leadership.

Cut off as they were from Russian society, the members of the

90

*Envoy Extraordinary*

Embassy staff, like those from other countries, were thrust back on their professional colleagues. The diplomatic corps occupied itself mainly in lunching and dining at other embassies and entertaining their members in return. Outside their comfortable prisons the vast catastrophic world of international politics heaved and roared like a menacing ocean, but the diplomatic corps was as much divorced from it as the occupants of a luxury cruise-boat. In her book *From Fear Set Free*, Nayantara Sahgal called their Moscow life 'as graceful, unreal and two-dimensional as a decorative gilded Byzantine canvas'.

Business was conducted through an organization known as 'Burobin', appointed by the Soviet Government to look after the embassies, which did not reply to urgent letters for weeks on end. But Vijaya Lakshmi, like the rest, found that business had to be created rather than confronted. For her it was largely confined to the safe cultural plane, such as organizing an Exhibition of Indian art, and bringing over Indian dancers for the entertainment of Soviet citizens.

The Indian Embassy, being new and modestly endowed as befitted a 'have-not' country, had a staff of only seventeen members which included everybody—diplomats, non-diplomats, and domestic workers. By contrast the British and American Embassies were overwhelming and splendid, exuberantly advertising their wealth to the critical Communist society which surrounded them; Washington had sent to Moscow a staff of 400 which included a doctor and a dentist. But Vijaya Lakshmi's small dining-room, adorned by colourful and original table-decorations created largely from vegetables cut to resemble flowers (which were expensive), made up in friendliness for its freedom from pomp. She often entertained her staff of young clerks and stenographers to dinner, when everybody sang and imported, with the songs, their own Indian world.

Outside the Embassies, shabby, pale-faced women, heroic and untidy, with faces untouched by cosmetics, endlessly besieged the shops, which could sell only bare necessities, and carried home their small bundles. They were paying, and would pay for many more years, for Russia's scientific civilization and its subsequent achievements. It was perhaps her knowledge of their sacrifices which led Vijaya Lakshmi to say at a Foyles' luncheon in London in April 1961, soon after the first Soviet space flight, that she wondered whether the conquest of other worlds would add to the sum of human happiness while our own remained unconquered.

Yet Russian men and women, like the Indians, sang at their work, inspired by a determined faith in their uncertain but costly future.

## Soviet Citadel 91

They also went to the ballet and theatre in their heavy working clothes, the women wearing scarves round their heads, and were quick to applaud. The Pandit daughters joined the crowds at the Bolshoi Theatre, and marvelled at the contrast between the fantastic brilliance of the ballet and the austere business of everyday living. They also recognized a kinship between the customs of Soviet Asia which contributed to the ballet's setting, and the vivid *décor* of Indian drama.

In summer Vijaya Lakshmi took a *dacha* outside the city where Lecky and Tara walked with their friends beneath the awe-inspiring trees of the Russian forest, and organized picnics at which they ate black bread, cheese and sausages, and drank Russian wine. After years of exacting political work, their mother found that she had time to read and think, and get acquainted with her colleagues. If she was cut off by adamant regulations from friendships with the Soviet citizens to whose country she had been accredited, she could at least rediscover the culture of Europe at the embassies, and study China in terms of the long-established Chinese Ambassador, Dr Fu. (What became of him, she often wondered, after the establishment of the Chinese People's Republic just after she left Moscow?)

Yet when she returned to India for a visit, her daughters discovered a characteristic ability to transform the unknown and remote Russians into human personalities, with all the variations and exasperations of humanity, for the benefit of fascinated listeners in Allahabad. She talked to them especially of the Russian women, who far from being socially linked with their husbands as in Britain and the United States, mingled chiefly with the groups into which their professional qualifications and interests took them. Lawyers associated with lawyers, engineers with engineers, and none of them worried about 'feminine charm', though quite a few possessed it.

Even in this equal society, Vijaya Lakshmi found that one of her chief problems arose from her position as a woman Ambassador. Being both the Ambassador and the Ambassador's wife, she had to accept social calls from either sex in the diplomatic hierarchy. And should she, at official dinners, retire to the drawing-room with the women, or remain with the men enjoying their drinks and cigars? In the end, determined by the prestige of her assignment, she wisely decided to stay. At her next diplomatic post, in Washington, she found that she was expected to join the women, and to leave a senior official to act as host to the men.

Reviewing both periods in retrospect, she decided that socially she had been the Ambassador in Moscow, but the Ambassador's wife in

## 92    *Envoy Extraordinary*

Washington. She naturally preferred the former status; the Russians, she said, always gave her a fair deal because they treated her as a diplomat, and not as a woman or even a nice woman. They would send for her at 11 p.m. exactly as they sent for other heads of missions. At her television interview with Ludovic Kennedy in July 1961, she explained that the 'disadvantage' of being a woman lay entirely in the minds of those with whom she had to deal.

'For instance, with the Russians my sex made no difference. The Americans never could accept me as anything but a woman.'

Before she left Moscow, new regulations caused the guards at the doors of all the embassies to be doubled. 'Suspicion,' reports Nayantara Sahgal in *From Fear Set Free*, 'had filtered down to kindergarten level.' She relates how the six-year-old son of India's cultural attaché, asked by a classmate if his father was a Communist, had replied with resourceful intelligence, rooted in a literary upbringing: 'Of course not. He's a Checkovist.'

But the Russian attitude to India had in fact become colder. Long afterwards Vijaya Lakshmi related that towards the end of her assignment she was 'dropped' by the Russians because the Indian mission did not go as far to the left as Moscow had hoped after her spectacular performance at the United Nations, where revolution was in the air.

'When I first arrived,' she told the *Manchester Guardian* correspondent in May 1948, 'I was very well received by the Russians. I was "the lady who won that brilliant victory over South Africa at the UN". But on the whole we are not having as many contacts with the Russians as I hoped we should have.'

She added a shrewd summary of the Soviet estimate of India.

'I think that the average educated Russian knows a good deal more about India than the same kind of people in many other countries. But this applies mostly to past Indian history. I know what the Marxist interpretation of India is—"the Indian people continue to be exploited by their bourgeoisie". Also, at the time of Gandhi's death there was a tendency to say that now Gandhi was dead, India would more than ever fall back on the British. Altogether I have found a tendency to dismiss us and our efforts as being of little consequence, and to identify us too much with Britain, and not to take enough notice of our leader's desire to build up an independent foreign policy, which is so important in South-eastern Asia.'

Mahatma Gandhi had been assassinated in January 1948, killed by a Hindu fanatic for seeking reconciliation with the Muslims, who

## Soviet Citadel 93

mourned him as one of themselves. When Vijaya Lakshmi heard the news, she grieved less for the unique exponent of non-violence, now immortalized by martyrdom, than for her brother. Lonely always on his solitary eminence, Jawaharlal, with Kamala and Ranjit dead, his daughter absorbed by her two small sons, and herself so far away, was now alone indeed. With Gandhi had gone his last strong link with the past; in the future he would himself carry the burden of the godhead which the Indian masses worshipped in their leaders, and which would cause him after his own death to be revered as semi-divine.

Later Vijaya Lakshmi learned how another great Indian had confronted the tragedy of Gandhi's death. On the day of his funeral Sarojini Naidu, now looking an old woman with the responsibility for 60 million people on her shoulders as Governor of the United Provinces, appeared at Delhi in mourning garments and addressed the Congress in the golden words of her matchless oratory.

'The time is over for private sorrow. The time is over for beating of breasts and tearing of hair. The time is here and now to stand up and say: "We take up the challenge with those who defied Mahatma Gandhi! We are his living symbols. We are the carriers of his banner before an embattled world! Our banner is truth, our shield is non-violence, our sword is the sword of the spirit that conquers without a blow! Shall we not follow in the footsteps of our master? Shall we not obey the mandates of our father? Though his voice will not speak again, have we not a million, million voices to bear his message to the world? Here and now I—for one—before the world that listens to my quivering voice, pledge myself as I did more than thirty years ago to the service of the Mahatma!

' "Mahatma Gandhi—whose frail body was committed to the flames today—is not dead! May the soul of my master, my leader, my father, rest *not* in peace! *Not* in peace—my father—do not rest! Keep us to our pledge! Give us strength to fulfil her promises—your heirs, your descendants, guardians of your dreams, fulfillers of India's destiny!" '

Thirteen months later, on March 1, 1949, Sarojini herself died of a heart attack after three week's illness. Four days earlier Dr Syud Hossain, Vijaya Lakshmi's distinguished San Francisco Chairman, had been found dead, also of heart failure, in his suite at Shepheard's Hotel in Cairo.[1] He had been India's Ambassador to Egypt since March 1948.

Weighed down by the loss of two such valuable friends and sup-

---

[1] February 25, 1949.

## 94 *Envoy Extraordinary*

porters, Vijaya Lakshmi returned from Russia to serve as India's Ambassador in Washington. It was one of her country's key diplomatic posts, which compelled her, as she had been compelled in the months following Ranjit's death, to put personal sorrows ruthlessly aside.

CHAPTER 8

# Washington Embassy

ON April 2 1949, Vijaya Lakshmi arrived in London from Moscow on her way to India for Chandalekha's marriage. Before leaving for her post in the United States, she had an interview at the Prime Minister's official residence with Robert Trumbull, the Delhi correspondent of the *New York Times*.

She told Mr Trumbull that her purposes as Ambassador to Washington were threefold. First, she hoped that her policy would lead to a combination of India's non-violent spirit with America's great material strength, and bring the realization that India's desire to avoid entanglement in the Cold War was not a weak, 'negative' purpose, but courageous and positive. Secondly, she wanted to make India, and Asia as a whole, better understood in the United States, and the United States more realistically appreciated in India, where the concept of American life had been too much influenced by Hollywood. She would like to see as many American students in India as there were Indians (then about 2,000) in American universities.

Thirdly, she would endeavour to promote American aid for India's vast and potentially rich territory, Having represented India in San Francisco and later at Lake Success, and having lectured in twenty-three States, she felt confident of coming closer to the Americans than she had been able to get to the Russians. She saw the job of an Ambassador as something much wider than just 'being a link between my government and the government to which I am accredited, for a good Ambassador could do so much to create understanding. In the West, for example, Gandhi was so often described as "an enigma", but he was fully understood by Indians, whom he had led such a long way towards the kindlier philosophy of the Buddha's epoch.'

She added that she was a firm proponent of India's return to her own inheritance, as opposed to a cheap imitation of the West.

'We must keep our roots in our own culture. Take my life as an example. I can't remember when I could not speak English—I had a

# 96      *Envoy Extraordinary*

European upbringing. If the emphasis had been on my own traditions and culture, I would be in a position today to contribute much more.'

The new Ambassador reached the United States at the end of April as the successor to Sir Benegal Rama Rau, who had been appointed to Washington on June 18, 1948, but had now left to become Governor of the Reserve Bank of India. Concurrently she was appointed Ambassador to Mexico as soon as personnel and materials were available for the establishment of a mission. Accompanied by Rita, then nineteen, she was greeted in New York by thirty representatives of Indian organizations, who presented her with two garlands and a bouquet. She insisted that she was not impressed by being the first woman Ambassador to the United States, for diplomatic and other posts should be assigned on the basis of ability, not of sex. More important, as an augury for world peace, was the recent lifting of the Berlin blockade by the Russians.

After a few days at the Ritz-Carlton Hotel, New York, she arrived on May 9th in Washington, where the British Ambassador and his wife, Sir Oliver (now Lord) and Lady Franks, met her at the airport.

'To greet her as she stepped from the plane,' recorded the *New York Times* for May 10th, 'was one of the largest crowds of US officials, foreign diplomats and countrymen ever to meet an arriving Ambassador.'

Two days later she called on President Truman to present her credentials. The Press reported that she wore a silver-blue sari for the occasion. Soon afterwards the White House formally announced that Mr Nehru had accepted the President's invitation to visit the United States in October.

Vijaya Lakshmi found the Indian Embassy established in a small though elegant residential house in a wooded area near Rock Creek Park. It faced imposing Massachusetts Avenue across a sober triangle of grass, which agreeably cut it off from the worst clamour of the noisy traffic. Modest and unpretentious, with a quiet high-ceilinged lounge, it had none of the impressive spaciousness of London's India House.[1]

Here, in June 1949, Vijaya Lakshmi held her first Press conference, which drew an overflow crowd of Washington journalists. One of them inevitably reported that she wore a purple sari and sandals.

---

[1] When I called at this embassy early in 1964, the lounge had a white ceiling and pale green walls. A large oblong mirror hung over the mantelpiece, where a golden elephant was the only adornment. This elephant, and a number of Indian ornaments within a semi-circular glass case, caught the spring sunlight vividly shining through the still bare trees.

V.B.

## Washington Embassy 97

According to Josephine Ripley, the correspondent of the *Christian Science Monitor*, she made a favourable impression from the outset.

'If India is counting on its new Ambassador to the United States to make friends and influence people, it is not likely to be disappointed. Completely without pose, affectation, or feminine mannerisms, she handled questions with what appeared to be perfect frankness, but was quick to detect and parry the "loaded" ones.'

By now Vijaya Lakshmi had become familiar with Press questions which sought to make political capital out of the prolonged tension between India and Britain. When she was asked how long she had been in jail, she said that if the question had any connection with British rule in India she would rather not reply. She gave the information only when assured that the reporter merely wanted to refresh his memory. To the usual inquiry how far it was a help or a handicap in her job to be a woman, she answered that women in India did not use their 'femininity' to promote political progress. Owing to her country's religious tradition, Indian women had taken their work seriously and with humility, and were not dependent on dress or make-up to emphasize their influence.

More difficult than parrying the customary inquiries was the task of convincing this crowd of hard-boiled American reporters that India was not a nation of 'fellow-travellers', but was sincerely dedicated to the cause of world peace and the freedom of subject races, which could only be achieved 'if we maintain a stand of aloofness from power blocs'. She assured the Press that she saw no present danger of Communism in India; 'the Communist Party there is small, has grown weaker in the past year, has only a nuisance value, and is not a menace'. Later, after the establishment of the Chinese People's Republic, she came to be involved in frequent conflict with Washington officials who regarded India's prompt recognition of Communist China as a betrayal of the 'free world', and viewed India's policy of non-alignment between East and West with angry suspicion.

As she stood up, an expert fencer, to the questions and comments with which the experienced Washington newspapermen tried to disconcert her, not one ever suspected the underlying flood of private sorrow which eddied, a dark tempestuous torrent, beneath the shining surface of her public life. When Iqbal Singh wrote in India's *Illustrated Weekly* for November 18, 1956, of 'the rare combination of fortunate circumstances and influences which have played a part in moulding her sensibility . . . We think, not without a degree of envious wonder, of

G

# 98 Envoy Extraordinary

the rich and strange background provided by the Nehru household', it was only that shining surface which he saw.

The political climate of Washington made it difficult to insist on the more unpopular aspects of her country's policy. In 1945 the Americans had been wholly sympathetic to Indian ambitions, and now expected that, after this moral support, India would side with the United States on every issue. They could not understand her wanting her own point of view, which was that 'containment' and 'non-alignment' were incompatible.

Personal friendship and growing esteem for Vijaya Lakshmi herself were thus combined with a deep distrust of India's motives; in consequence Indo-American relations were strained, and her position as Ambassador was delicate and complicated. She sometimes felt that the Indian Government really had not developed a firm policy towards the United States. It was a topic that she would have liked to discuss with her brother, but the opportunity seemed never to occur. To these problems had to be added the complete failure of the Soviet Union to give her any diplomatic experience. The only lesson learnt there was the conduct of relationships with other foreign missions; there had been little to teach her how to deal with the government to which she was accredited.

In its own peculiar way the Washington of 1949 was almost as difficult as Stalin's intransigent Moscow. It was insular and protocol-ridden, and had little society to offer outside that of the diplomatic corps, the State Department, and the Senators—of whom too many were ignorant and sometimes bigoted. Among such officials her position as a woman brought uncomfortable dilemmas. American male diplomats cherished an unshakeable conviction that a woman's version of the facts was anyhow bound to be wrong, and at first the State Department made a habit of sending their own reports to India as a check on hers—an impertinence of which they would never have been guilty had she been a man.

Initially they had been more impressed by her status as Jawaharlal Nehru's sister, and by the regal manner acquired from her princess-like upbringing, than by her genuine and hard-earned political experience. She proved, however, to be a quick and intelligent learner, and by the time she left Washington was widely acknowledged to be at least as able as the best of her predecessors in the India Section of the State Department.

'Outside Washington,' she admitted years afterwards, 'I found many friends and it was through them that I learned to love America. Had I

# Washington Embassy

known only Washington, I would never have been drawn to the United States.' But gradually she did come to realize that America herself was greater than all but one or two really fine individuals such as Mrs Roosevelt; as a nation she gave enormous help to other less privileged countries after the Second World War.

The first major event of Vijaya Lakshmi's Ambassadorship was her brother's visit to the United States in October 1949. He had never been in America before, and described his journey as 'a voyage of discovery'. Among many minor addresses he made two important speeches, the first in Washington to the House of Representatives and the Senate, and the second in New York on October 19th to a combined meeting of the East and West Association, the Foreign Policy Association, the India League of America, and the Institute of Pacific Relations. For the second he was expected to prepare a written address but instead, apologizing for his failure to make a set speech which 'I am not used to doing in India', he gave them 'a friendly talk' which arose, he said, from his growing sense of confidence in American friendship.

In the first speech he compared the American and Indian revolutions,[1] drawing attention to certain likenesses between the Declaration of Independence and the Constitution of the Republic of India.[2] He closed with a reference to India's need for economic aid, since 'political freedom without the assurance of the right to live and to pursue happiness which economic progress alone can bring, can never satisfy a people.' He added that the objects of India's foreign policy were 'the preservation of world peace and enlargement of human freedom.'

During the address at the banquet in New York, after acknowledging the help given by the United States to India's pursuit of independence and to the formal inauguration of the Indian Republic three months hence, he made, in discussing India's land problem, one of his rare references to Vijaya Lakshmi's achievements.

---

[1] My husband and I possess a picture of Thomas Jefferson which Mr Nehru signed on the reverse side at our request during a visit to England shortly before the Second World War.

V.B.

[2] Of this he quoted the Preamble:
'We, the people of India, having solemnly resolved to constitute India into a Sovereign Democratic Republic, and to secure to all its citizens:
Justice, social, economic and political;
Liberty of thought, expression, belief, faith and worship;
Equality of status and of opportunity, and to promote among them all
Fraternity assuring the dignity of the individual and the unity of the Nation;
In our Constituent Assembly do hereby adopt, enact and give to ourselves this Constitution.'

# Envoy Extraordinary

'In my own province in India, that is, the United Provinces, which is the biggest province and has the enormous population of about 60 millions, we introduced a great reform in local self-government. In all the villages, a vast number of villages, every adult voted in what was probably one of the biggest elections that any country has had. We are going to have that all over India. That particular reform in local self-government, affecting all the villages, was really initiated some years ago when my sister, who is our Ambassador here, was the Minister for local self-government in that province. Now, this is an extraordinary and a most interesting experiment. Partly it is new. Partly it is going back to village self-government that existed before the British came.[1]

Anyhow, it is a tremendous experiment in democracy, important perhaps because it is more basic than the Assembly that we may choose the top.'

He concluded by saying that he would go back to India much richer than he came, and especially in the intellectual and emotional understanding and appreciation of the American people. Thus he amply fulfilled the expectation which Vijaya Lakshmi had voiced to President Truman: 'His visit will help the American people to become more aware of India, and I hope he will take back a greater awareness of the people of America.'

An important mitigating factor in the Ambassador's heavy obligations soon came to be the growing respect and friendship of Mr Dean Acheson, the Secretary of State, who was entirely frank with her. Like other members of the State Department he admired her uninhibited opposition to Krishna Menon, never a favourite with America owing to his supposed Communist proclivities. This opposition, however, really came to the surface when her diplomatic mission to Washington was over, and Menon replaced her as the leader of the Indian Delegation to the United Nations in 1953.

Menon, enigmatic, brilliant, Mephistophelean, a unique compound of courage and bitterness, had been, since Independence, India's first High Commissioner in the United Kingdom after some twenty years of residence in London.[2] To Vijaya Lakshmi he was an unwelcome symbol of power since she deplored his influence over Jawaharlal, who regarded Menon as the only person close to him with a real comprehen-

---

[1] See Chapter 3, p. 49.

[2] He was appointed after some protest by the Attlee Government, and remained in the London post until Mr B. G. Kher succeeded him on June 13, 1952.

## Washington Embassy

sion of his thinking.[1] This influence was one of several difficult family problems in the background of her life. The lack of real affection, perhaps rooted in jealousy, between her younger sister and herself represented another. But most painful of all was the complex relationship with her brother, once her uncriticized hero, from whom she now often differed in her estimates of persons and events. When combined with her tormenting devotion to him, these disagreements, whether major or minor, were a source of continuous distress.[2]

Even without such personal complications, her task of maintaining friendly Indo-American relations was difficult enough in terms of contrary political valuations combined with India's overwhelming economic needs. On June 12, 1952, in a debate on Foreign Affairs in India's Lok Subha (Lower House), Mr Nehru was to outline the pattern within which the Indian Ambassador to Washington had to operate.

'It has repeatedly been said that we incline more and more towards the Anglo-American bloc. It is perfectly true that during the last few years we have had more economic and other bonds with the United Kingdom and the United States of America than with other countries. That is a situation we have inherited and unless we develop new bonds we shall have to continue as we are doing. That some people obsessed by passion and prejudice disapprove of our relations with the Anglo-American bloc is not sufficient reason for us to break any bond which is of advantage to us. A country, placed as India is today, has inevitably to depend on other countries for certain essential things. We are not industrialized enough to produce all that we need . . . Of course, we must try to build up basic industries so that we can produce things for our essential needs, but what are we to do in the meantime? We have to get them from those countries where our existing economic contacts make it easier for us to do so.'

Between 1949 and 1951 the three major problems of Indo-American diplomacy were the Wheat Loan Agreement, the Japanese Peace

[1] According to the biography of Menon by T. J. S. George (Cape, 1964), the mutual relationship between Jawaharlal Nehru and Menon was very close, and Mr Nehru's decision to keep India in the Commonweath was largely due to Menon's influence and legalistic ingenuity. It is probably impossible for any Westerner to understand Menon sufficiently to do him justice. Those who wish to make the attempt should read Mr George's book, written with relative detachment in spite of his evident admiration for his subject.

[2] This emerged with especial clarity from the article entitled *Nehru and Madame Pandit*, 'by their sister Krishna Nehru Hutheesing', published by the *Ladies' Home Journal* (USA) in January 1955.

## 102        *Envoy Extraordinary*

Treaty and the Korean War, which began on June 15, 1950, three years after the problem of Korean independence had been brought before the General Assembly of the United Nations. With the Japanese Treaty, debated at an historic Conference in San Francisco, Vijaya Lakshmi had no vital connection. The Korean War, which in Mr Nehru's words in Parliament on October 3, 1950, had in it 'the seeds of a mighty conflict' and laid down for many years the Cold War pattern of East-West relations, did not closely involve India until August 1953, and her attitude to it remained cautious throughout.

By the time that India furnished the 6,000 troops who acted as guards during the difficult post-Armistice period when the voluntary repatriation of prisoners took place,[1] Vijaya Lakshmi had ceased to be Ambassador to Washington, though she was still at her post on July 30, 1951, when the negotiations began for a truce along the 38th Parallel. But she held a key position in relation to the Wheat Loan negotiations, which represented a main feature of the Indian Government's economic policy.

Her problem was that of obtaining the much-needed grain without loss of the prestige so important to a newly independent country. Tragic though its implications were in terms of half-starved Indians dying from undernourishment, the negotiations themselves involved a 'comic opera' situation. India wanted wheat, but did not want to ask for it either as a loan or a gift. The Americans possessed wheat in abundance and were anxious to give it away, but were not prepared to make this gesture except on request.

Since Vijaya Lakshmi's Ambassadorship ended in 1951, just when India's First Five-Year Plan for economic development was initially laid down, she had to negotiate the Agreement before India's desire to stand economically on her own feet became evident to the world through the Plan's publication. Her difficulty was thus much greater than that of her successors making comparable arrangements after India, by taxing herself to the limit and accepting a level of austerity inconceivable to the West, had given proof of her determination to contribute to her own economic independence.[2]

Finally Vijaya Lakshmi sent a judiciously-worded note asking for the wheat, but not specifying whether a gift or a loan was expected. The Americans agreed, and the grain, worth some 30 million dollars,

---

[1] The Indian troops finally went home in February 1954.
[2] Within ten years of the Wheat Loan negotiations, India had increased her *per capita* income by $13 a year (from $52 to $65), with something less than 3 per cent in terms of aid from other countries.

## Washington Embassy

was eventually provided. Soon afterwards the first shipment left from Florida, and with appropriate ceremony she witnessed its departure. For her diplomatic skill she received the 'omnibus' acknowledgment to which she was now accustomed.[1]

'I want to say very clearly,' Jawaharlal commented in Parliament on December 7, 1950, 'that we have been served very well by our Ambassadors at Lake Success, in Washington, in London, in Peking, and in Moscow.'

Mr Nehru's visit to the United States was soon followed by another of a more domestic variety. Within the preceding twelve months not only Lekha but Tara had married; both girls were now expecting babies. During a flying visit to India in the winter of 1949–50, their mother commented that every girl should have her first baby in her parents' home, and invited Tara and her husband, Gautam Sahgal, to visit her in Washington. When both commented that America was a long way to travel from Kanpur to have a baby, Vijaya Lakshmi merely responded: 'Unless we're never going to meet, you'll have to get used to travelling long distances to see me.'

When the visit finally took place Mr Sahgal, who had little enthusiasm for the trip, violently reacted, like many other 'aliens', against having his finger and palm prints taken at the American Embassy in Delhi. Tara also found the experience disconcerting, since she afterwards remembered nothing whatsoever about her daughter's birth in a Washington hospital—an omission drastically remedied the following year when her son Ranjit was born in Allahabad.[2]

The visit proved, however, to be of practical use to both young women, since Vijaya Lakshmi totally disregarded the careful lists of baby clothes furnished by both her expectant daughters, and characteristically provided for all their maternal needs from weighing machines to nappies. Actually her daughter and son-in-law saw little of her, for her life in Washington kept her constantly on the move; she was obliged to fulfil speaking engagements all over the country, and had no time to attend the International Mother of the Year Luncheon at the Waldorf-Astoria in New York in May 1950.

Her award as 'Mother of the Year' for India was one of many tributes which Vijaya Lakshmi received from the United States during her period as Ambassador. These included six honorary Doctor of Law Degrees from American colleges and universities, including Wellesley

---

[1] The payment for this wheat is still outstanding, but India's *amour-propre* remains undiminished owing to the fact that it has never been officially acknowledged as a gift.

[2] *From Fear Set Free*, p. 132.

104 *Envoy Extraordinary*

College; several citations from national organizations; the honorary Presidency of the Indian Division of the Asia Institute; a Medallion as 'Outstanding Woman of the Year 1949' from the Women's International Exposition, New York; and nomination as one of seventeen 'Women of Achievement' by the American Federation of Soroptimist Clubs.

When she found that she could not attend the Mother of the Year Luncheon, she urged Tara to take her place. Tara, nearing the birth of her baby, attended the glittering ceremony with understandable reluctance, but recovered her poise when the Mother for Pakistan turned out to be a male official with a luxuriant black moustache uncomfortably representing his wife.

Although India's desire to establish a mission in Mexico became well known as soon as Vijaya Lakshmi arrived in Washington, she was still awaiting a 'gesture' from the Mexicans at the beginning of 1951. Mexico had not yet named a representative to India, though President Miguel Aleman's recent formal acknowledgment of Mrs Pandit as India's envoy established the initial diplomatic relationship between the two countries, and made her the first woman to hold two Ambassadorships simultaneously.

Mexico and India, she told the Press, had worked well together at the United Nations, and shared the same opinion regarding Korea and other international questions. They had much experience to give each other of world importance, especially in studying the problems of rural areas, and had launched the same type of 'literacy campaign' by which each literate person taught from one to three other individuals to read and write during school and college vacations. India, which had one of the largest motion picture industries in the world, planned to send new films to Mexico, and also to hold an exhibition of Indian art there at which Indian dancers would appear.

Finally, early in the year, the summons came, and she left by air for Mexico City on February 6, 1951. It was her first trip to Latin America, and at Washington Airport before leaving she took the opportunity in a formal statement of making clear the difference of opinion between India and the United States regarding the recognition of newly-established Communist China.

India realized, she observed judiciously, that her goal for a democratic peaceful world, with India as the bulwark of Asia, was merely a different approach from that of the United States in achieving the same purpose. She added that India was a constitutional democracy and a secular state.

## Washington Embassy 105

'There are as many different points of view in our Republic as there are in yours. On foreign policy there is basic agreement. This policy is pro-United Nations and pro-free nations. We deplore the word "neutralism" as applied to us in our situation. We are members of the United Nations and we stand with you for freedom, equality, orderly justice, and for a world at peace. India opposes every form of imperialism whether economic or any other kind.'[1]

To a question put by Ludovic Kennedy, on the contrast between Russia and China during his broadcast interview with Vijaya Lakshmi on July 16, 1961[2], she admitted that the relationship between India and China was not as close as it had been, and continued: 'But I do feel that Russia is trying much harder to evolve a pattern of peace than China.'

At this interview, ten years after she left Washington and could see her mission there in perspective, he put several questions regarding the contrast between Russia and America in her own experience. She replied frankly that though the United States itself was full of interest, she had to work within a pattern that did not appeal to her, and left little scope for applying her own knowledge.

Because the Americans could never accept her as anything but a woman, they adopted a special attitude towards her when discussing political questions.

'They were always a little chivalrous, a little polite, and probably I got away with more than I could have done if I'd been a man.' She said of her subsequent experience in Britain: "It was something like that in the beginning here.'

In a private discussion two years later, she added that she had constantly to side-step irrelevances—not the least of these being the tendency of Americans, and especially of American reporters, to

---

[1] Since the period covered by this chapter, relations between Washington and Delhi appear to have changed significantly. After the Chinese invasion of 1962 a greater sense of obligation to the United States developed in India, and a less resolute policy of non-alignment. Contemporary Indian records of the Korean War appeared to be unobtainable in Washington in March 1964, and are probably no longer there. Though it was the chief political event of 1949–51, a former State Department official suggested to the author that the whole episode was probably regarded as a past happening best forgotten. Owing, however, to the cautious attitude maintained by India throughout the war, he thought it unlikely that speeches giving uncritical support to China had been made by any Indian. The belief that China, as a *de facto* great power, should be a member of the United Nations was, and is, a totally different question.

[2] i.e. before the Chinese invasion.

106            *Envoy Extraordinary*

describe her clothes rather than her policy.[1] She continued by saying
that in her opinion the American belief in sex equality was entirely
theoretical. American diplomats had tried to 'edge her out' of diplomatic opportunities, especially in after-dinner discussions. It was the
Norwegian Ambassador who insisted on her remaining at the dinner
tables and kept everybody there.

At a Glasgow reception in 1955, she had already permitted herself
some truthful comments.

'When my public activities are reported it is very annoying to read
how I looked, if I smiled, if a particular reporter like my hair style.'
Though she had been nervous about her ability to discharge her duties
in the Soviet Union, she confirmed previous statements that she was
treated throughout as the Ambassador for India 'and that was all.
But when I went to Washington, from the day I went to the day I left,
I was continually trying to convince people I was the Ambassador from
India and nobody else. I was "honey" to so many people, and it does
rather detract from things when you come to discuss some very
important matter which the Government has entrusted to you.'[2]

To a further question by Ludovic Kennedy on Moscow and
Washington—'I'm wondering . . . whether you think there's any
possibility of two countries with such totally different traditions and
cultures and outlooks and attitudes ever coming closer together', she
gave a frank reply which surprised him.

'You know, what happens to anybody who's been in these two
places and has looked at them objectively, is the horrifying thought—
if I may use that word in quotes—that they are so similar.'

To a request for further elucidation, she continued:

'Take that passion for science—they're both absolutely dedicated to
the machine, they are both extroverts, they both function in much the
same way; you see the Russians standing in the snow in their queues
waiting for their little ice-cream packets, just as you see the Americans
queuing up at their Howard Johnsons, or whatever it is, to eat the next
flavour of ice-cream. These are silly little things about food and so on.
But this thing about the machine and about their approach to life is
really remarkable, and if they should ever come together—of course
I know that an ocean separates the thinking between them—but if
they should ever come together, I think it might be in a very good way.'

[1] Even the able Robert Trumbull of the *New York Times*, in spite of a sympathetic
assessment of her purposes as Ambassador to Washington, felt impelled to add: 'She looks
as good in the sari as the sari looks on her'.
[2] *The Scotsman*, August 29, 1955.

## Washington Embassy 107

In response to his interruption—'Well, not only an ocean but a diametrically opposed political system', she retaliated: 'Sometimes, you know, extremes do meet. And one would like to feel they did for the sake of the rest of us. Because I do feel that there isn't going to be much security in our lives until some pattern is worked out to which both the USA and the USSR can contribute.'

In March 1951, Vijaya Lakshmi asked to be relieved of the Washington post in order to return to Indian politics and contest a seat in the United Provinces during the coming General Election. Bidding farewell at Washington's Union Station to Sir Oliver and Lady Franks on November 10, 1951, she was seen off from Idlewild Airport[1] by some twenty friends and members of her staff. She had been Ambassador to Washington for nearly three years, and remarked hopefully to the interviewing reporters that 'the United States and India's basic approaches to important problems have a great deal of similarity'.

[1] Now Kennedy Airport.

CHAPTER 9

# United Nations

In 1952 the newly emancipated people of India elected a government of their own choice for the first time in Indian history. Unlike the election of 1937 this one was not confined to British India, where the franchise had been determined by educational and property qualifications. Now every adult was going to vote, whether he or she possessed what the West calls 'a stake in the country' or not. Since most of the 180 millions of registered voters were still illiterate, they learnt to recognize their candidates by picturesque animal symbols. Vijaya Lakshmi covered the length and breadth of the country in that election, and subsequently commented that India would never have created her astonishing framework of democracy if she had waited for 360 million people to become literate. She expressed her astonishment just the same that such an election could have been organized on that vast scale without mishap.

At the upper end of the social hierarchy the 500 princely States previously omitted from the British administrative framework were not excluded, though most of the princes were still far from achieving psychological unity with the new-born country which they found so uncomfortable. Perhaps, it was thought, a General Election would help them to acquire a sense of identity with the half-fed, half-clad, underprivileged masses who were voting with them. As time went by an intelligent few among these aristocratic voters did achieve that identity, becoming deputies and even members of the Government.

In December 1951, Vijaya Lakshmi returned from Washington to stand for election. She found Allahabad, which was her brother's constituency, much changed since the Partition; many of the shops were now owned by refugee Punjabis. Nayantara Sahgal, in her book *From Fear Set Free*, has described how Jawaharlal Nehru arrived by plane from Delhi to speak at a huge public meeting, and drove into the portico of Anand Bhawan wearing the usual fresh rose in his button-

# United Nations 109

hole. His sister joined him, and the excited crowds, seized by election fever, inundated the house.

Before he set off to cover the vast dusty spaces dividing the cities in which he had set himself the task of educating the electorate, a conversation took place between him and Vijaya Lakshmi which Tara has recorded. When she urged her brother to behave 'like a human being, not a driven animal', and to allow himself some occasional relaxation, he answered quietly: 'There isn't time. We are here to work till we're thrown on the rubbish heap.' Angry with herself for being moved by his words, Vijaya Lakshmi retorted: 'You may be. I'm not. I'd like to see anyone throw me on any rubbish heap!' But after his death she sent to an old friend some lines by Robert Frost which he had kept on his work-table:

> 'The woods are lonely dark and deep
> But I have promises to keep
> And miles to walk before I sleep.'

Stirred by his speeches the people came out to vote, and eventually gave Vijaya Lakshmi one of the biggest majorities in all India. To the surprise of the world and even of India herself, more than 60 per cent of the women took part in this first General Election. Groups of women from rural areas flocked to the polls, eager to use their new power. Long ago, as India's first woman Minister in the United Provinces, Vijaya Lakshmi herself had begun the process of awakening their political consciousness.

Jawaharlal Nehru had in fact only another dozen years to live before his ashes were cast, not indeed on any rubbish heap, but upon India's sacred rivers as a symbol of his immortality. Though he was to achieve so much in those twelve years, he left, inevitably, much more to be accomplished, and may well have been justified in his feeling that to take any relaxation would be unfair to his successors.

For all the indignant candour of his sister's words, she took none either, and for most of that new decade was to drive herself to the point of breakdown at the superhuman task of being an effective High Commissioner in the United Kingdom. Now, in March 1952, she was summoned to another difficult assignment, shorter and less exacting but demanding the maximum of diplomatic discretion, for she was invited to lead the Indian Government's first goodwill mission to Communist China. During this visit, reported the *Christian Science Monitor* on October 26, 1953, she 'donned Chinese trousers and coat presented to her by Chou En-lai.'

110                    *Envoy Extraordinary*

Two years later, in a debate on Foreign Affairs in the Lok Sabha on September 29, 1954, Jawaharlal Nehru unequivocally expressed his thoughts on the world's attitude to China at that time:

'I have long been convinced of the fact that a great part of our present difficulties—certainly in the Far East, but I would like to go farther and say in the world—is due to this extraordinary shutting of one's eyes to the fact of China. It is totally immaterial whether you like China or dislike it ... I am convinced that there would have been no Korean War if the People's Government of China had been in the United Nations, because people could have dealt with China across the table.'

Vijaya Lakshmi had never shown any sympathy with Communism as such, but she shared her brother's views to the extent that, both in the United States and elsewhere, she had utterly refused to join the anti-Communist camp. This, she repeatedly made clear, was not because China was Communist, but because it was a great Asian power with the right to decide its own form of government.

Even in November 1962, after the Chinese invasion of the Sino-Indian frontier, she was still able to say at a London reception given for her by the YMCA Indian Students' Union:

'Nobody would have rejoiced more than I at the achievements of the new China. As a member of the Government delegation I spent a very interesting six weeks in China. We saw much that filled us with hope. We did not mind that their experiment was different from our own as we accepted that the strength of the world consisted in its diversity and that co-existence would have to be achieved. We said then that China and ourselves together would be a force for good in the years to come. So far our hopes have not matured, and we are unable to say today, as I have been saying, that over two thousand miles of common border we have had two thousand years of peace.'

In Bombay, the year after her tour, she spoke of her initial consciousness of China's immense revolutionary vitality. With many aspects of the People's Republic she was greatly impressed; among these were the cleanliness and order everywhere, the enthusiasm of the men and women whom her delegation met, and the unity of purpose which seemed to exist between the people and their rulers. China's most distinctive features, she added, seemed to her to be the method of education, and the manner in which the national drive behind the three 'antis'—anti-waste, anti-corruption, and anti-bureaucratism—was being carried out with an often frightening ruthlessness.

# United Nations

She had been alarmed too by the hate campaign against the United States, then at its height and very disturbing. This phenomenon was a consequence of the Korean War.

'The Chinese seemed to change suddenly from courteous hosts to frenzied animals when America was mentioned. They *hate* Americans. The Russians do not hate them in the same way. The Americans grieved because they had always loved and helped China.'

She had felt a great sense of pride in seeing another Asian country go ahead, and in 1962 was correspondingly disappointed. The measure of her brother's bitter disillusionment must have been wholly evident to her. Some Westerners who visited India at that time felt when Mr Nehru died eighteen months after the Chinese invasion that he was as much a victim of Chinese policy as any soldier who fell fighting on the frontier.

During her term as Ambassador to Moscow, Vijaya Lakshmi had been concurrently leader of the Indian delegation to the United Nations, and again filled this position in 1952–53. That year India had perhaps a more important function to perform than at previous Assemblies owing to her part in the plan for ending the Korean War. At this period Mr Chester Bowles, the American Ambassador to India, told Indian diplomats that the war's extension was inevitable unless a solution was reached soon. He suggested that India might take the lead in bringing the protracted negotiations to an end.

These had been going on since the summer of 1951, when the Soviet diplomat Jacob Malik suddenly announced that a cease-fire could be arranged. But as soon as the opposing sides began armistice discussions at Panmunjom, a number of complications arose. After months of inconclusive frustration most of the difficulties had been ironed out, but one major cause of stumbling remained: the future of the numerous prisoners of war.

Ever since war-prisoners became a subject for international negotiation after the Franco-Prussian War of 1870,[1] their fate had usually been a subject on which adversaries could agree. But after the Korean War the United Nations held some 140,000 prisoners, of whom many had made clear their objection to being repatriated.[2] The United Nations, dominated by the United States, therefore established the principle that prisoners should be allowed to decide their fate for themselves, while China and North Korea, technically supported by the 1949 Geneva

---

[1] Treaty of Frankfurt, May 10, 1871, Article X.
[2] The Communist side refused information about the numbers or condition of those in their hands.

112    *Envoy Extraordinary*

Convention, insisted that all prisoners should be repatriated whatever their inclinations. Owing to the deadlock over this unusual problem, the truce talks were suspended for the second time in October 1952.

At this point the Indian delegation—with Vijaya Lakshmi as its head for the fourth time,[1] and Krishna Menon as her reluctant second-in-command—arrived in New York for the opening session of the Seventh General Assembly. Among those representing Britain on this occasion was Mrs Evelyn Emmet (not yet a Member of Parliament), the first woman to be sent by the UK as a full delegate, though she was not Chairman. Another woman Chairman of a delegation was Dr Gertruda Sekaninova-Cakrtoya, the Deputy Foreign Minister of Czechoslovakia. New delegates included Begum Liaquat Ali Khan, later Pakistan's Ambassador at The Hague and afterwards in Rome.

Early in the proceedings Vijaya Lakshmi, who was now the acknowledged leader of the Arab-Asian bloc, categorically announced: 'An imperative duty is placed on us, who represent the coloured races of mankind, to remind this General Assembly that Africa and Asia are on the march and they will no longer accept the indignities imposed on them in the name of a white civilization.'

Almost immediately Krishna Menon, ignoring his dislike of a subordinate position, began his characteristic work of background lobbying. Those who seek to understand this baffling individual might perhaps ask themselves just how and why someone so apparently aggressive should use with such signal success the time-honoured methods of reconciliation. After weeks of feverish activity behind the scenes, Menon produced the 17-point 'Indian Plan', which upheld the American proposal of no forced repatriation while accepting the Communist idea that the fate of those prisoners who refused to go home should be decided at the peace conference to be held after the Armistice.

Immediately Russia's Andrei Vishinsky denounced India for having 'joined' the free world camp by accepting the principle of no forced repatriation. But eventually, after the full Assembly of the United Nations had passed the Indian Resolution in May 1953, the Communists at Panmunjom offered an 8-point plan that resembled the Indian Resolution flatly rejected by them five months earlier. India, in the person of Lieut.-General Thimayya, was now nominated Chairman and 'umpire' of the Neutral Nations Repatriation Commission.

On March 15, 1953, *Reynolds News* reported:

[1] The previous occasions had been in 1946, 1947 and 1948. She had attended the Fifth Session of the Status of Women Commission at Lake Success in 1951.

## United Nations 113

'At first the USA rejected out of hand the Indian plan on Korea last year. But the Indian leader refused to accept the situation. She set to work and by sheer tenacity, tact, and persuasive argument she won over the American Secretary of State, Mr Acheson. In the end the Indian Resolution was accepted by 54 member nations.'

This paragraph seems to ignore the skill and devotion of the unpopular Menon as completely as his biographer, Mr T. J. S. George, overlooks Vijaya Lakshmi's persistence and tactful persuasion. By the middle of March she was already being discussed as a possible Secretary-General in succession to Mr Trygve Lie, who announced his resignation after the Russian Government and its satellites had exerted, in his own words, 'the crudest possible pressure' against him since the outbreak of the Korean War. Other candidates nominated for the post were Mr Lester Pearson of Canada, General Romulo of the Philippines, and Mr Stanislaw Skrzesezewski of Poland, but Mr Dag Hammarskjoeld was eventually appointed.

On July 27th the Armistice was signed which concluded the Korean War. In the process of restoring the *status quo* to that of June 25, 1950, when the Communists invaded, the war had left 400,000 dead and made 4 million people homeless. Six weeks later, on September 17th, Andrei Vishinsky shook hands with Vijaya Lakshmi Pandit as the newly-elected President of the Eighth Assembly.

Her election as Lester Pearson's successor at this great gathering which, as her brother had said that spring,[1] represented 'the timeless urge of humanity for peace', was preceded by two hours of debate about the possible admission of Communist China. Eventually thirty-seven countries voted for Vijaya Lakshmi, and twenty-two for the only other candidate, Prince Wan Waithayakon, the head of the Siamese Delegation. Her supporters were understood to include the British Commonwealth (except South Africa), the Arab States, most of the Asian countries, Scandinavia, Israel, and some parts of Latin America.

According to the article by Iqbal Singh in India's *Illustrated Weekly* for November 18, 1956, her election at that critical period of the Cold War raised so many hopes that the UN Secretariat had to engage nine secretaries to deal with her mail—something that had not occurred before and has never happened since. As both a woman and an Indian she was regarded as peculiarly well qualified to bring a healing touch to existing pathological antagonisms. A story is told that when the Emir Feisal of Saudi Arabia passed her in the corridor he always bowed

---

[1] Speech in Lok Sabha, Delhi, February 18, 1953.

H

114 *Envoy Extraordinary*

his head, a tribute he did not pay to the other women delegates. When she once asked him the reason for this respectful treatment, he replied solemnly: 'Madame, they are women; you are my sister.'

On October 12, 1953, after publishing an article on the part played by women in India's national movement, the Editor of *Al Mussawar*, a leading Egyptian pictorial journal, wrote an 'open letter' to Vigjaya Lakshmi Pandit: 'We never expected anything good from the United Nations until the day you sat in its Presidential Chair. From you the nations will learn the meaning of wisdom, steadiness, and fair play. You will teach men that human love, the doctrine of the great leader Gandhi, is better fitted to bring happiness to the nations and to win friends than the Atom and Hydrogen bombs.'

Vijaya Lakshmi's colleagues knew that she would also be the most democratic and informal of Presidents, having many qualities in common with Eleanor Roosevelt. At previous UN sessions she had often been seen going to the Press cafeteria on the third floor, collecting a tray, and queueing for a sandwich and a cup of coffee. Later, when as High Commissioner to the United Kingdom she was presenting the prizes for the *Encyclopaedia Britannica* Press pictures of the year, and found one prize named after the late Hector McNeil, she recalled her acquaintanceship with him at the United Nations. Their Governments, she said, had registered them both at impressive hotels but failed to allow them enough spending money for the costly hotel breakfast, so they walked together each day to a modest coffee bar 'round the corner'.

Now, following her election, wearing a mauve sari trimmed with gold which the Press did not fail to describe, she moved quietly into the Presidential chair between Dag Hammarskjoeld and his executive assistant Andrew Cordier, and faced the delegates of sixty nations. These included her own delegation, led by Krishna Menon and Mrs Lakshmi Menon,[1] but amid general applause she formally dissociated herself from these colleagues and guaranteed complete impartiality as President.

'You choice is a tribute to my country,' she said, 'and a recognition of its profound desire to serve the purposes of the United Nations and through them the paramount interests of world peace. It is also a recognition of the part that women have played and are playing in furthering the aims and the purposes of this great organization.'

Her election was followed by a long discussion involving an amendment to the Charter proposed by the United States, which wished to

[1] Now Minister of State. She is not related to Krishna Menon.

# United Nations

remove from it the principle of the unanimity of the five permanent members of the Security Council. Jacob Malik, the Soviet delegate who was President of the Security Council that year, argued against this proposal at considerable length, and was supported by the Polish and Ukranian delegates. When Mr Van Balluseck of the Netherlands, Mr Lodge of the United States, and Mr Badawi of Egypt had spoken in favour of the proposal, Mr Malik returned to his argument with Mr Lodge.

As he was out of order by resuming the debate after three representatives on each side had been allowed to speak, Vijaya Lakshmi immediately turned a switch which cut off the Russian translation system. Realizing that he was now reduced to addressing the Assembly in a language which few delegates could understand, he turned round angrily saying 'That is why I oppose this item', and strode off the platform.

The new President continued calmly: 'We have now heard three speakers in favour of and three speakers against the inclusion of these items. I shall therefore put to the vote the recommendation of the General Council for the inclusion of items 70 and 72.' When the vote was taken the American proposal was placed on the Agenda by 51 votes to 5, with one abstention. Already Vijaya Lakshmi had demonstrated to the international world her capacity for swift decision. Subsequently any delegate who exceeded his or her time was turned off with a cordial smile and a sharp rap of the gavel formally presented to her by Mrs Roosevelt.

In August 1955 an article by Ela Sen in *Housewife* described Vijaya Lakshmi as 'impatient in rather a mannish way, which sits incongruously with her delicate femininity . . . It is difficult for her to suffer fools'. Jacob Malik was of course no fool, but a very adroit opponent who could be countered only by equal adroitness. It was perhaps of him amongst others that she was thinking when she said later of that autumn's experience that 'a glimpse of the inner tactics of politicians was at times rather disheartening and harassing'.

Although she had said of India's satisfaction at her appointment: 'The fact that I am a woman will be taken in their stride', she could at least remark on the improvement in the position of women at the United Nations which coincided with her Presidency. Though women were accepted in theory, there had been in practice few women on the delegations, and these were mostly 'advisers' or alternative delegates. Usually they functioned chiefly on certain Committees officially considered suitable for them, such as the Social and Human Rights Com-

116                     *Envoy Extraordinary*

mittees. There had never been a woman on the Political Committee apart from the leader of the Czech delegation for a short period in 1952 and Vijaya Lakshmi herself, steadily becoming the symbol of a future society which would recognize that woman's contribution, modifying the aggressive patterns laid down by man, was essential to human survival.

'I have a feeling, and I hope it may be proved wrong,' she said the year after her election, 'that if there is ever another woman President of the United Nations she will be from Asia.'

Though Europe was, on this record, so far behind Asia in its notions of sex equality, women had nevertheless doubled their ranks in the two previous years. Apart from Vijaya Lakshmi herself, twenty-six were now serving on national delegations, half as full delegates. They were jurists, legislators, and world leaders first, and women second. An illustration in the *Christian Science Monitor* for October 26, 1953, showed seventeen women at the United Nations. Besides Vijaya Lakshmi and Mrs Menon of India, they included Miss Minerva Bernadino of the Dominican Republic, Mrs Frances Bolton of the United States, and Mrs Evelyn Emmet of Great Britain.

'These women,' wrote the *Monitor*'s correspondent, Mary Hornaday, 'help to calm the atmosphere in this "workshop for peace" . . . Some of them complained about being herded into the Third Committee dealing with Social Welfare.'

On the other side of the world an article by Ava B. Wadia in India's monthly magazine *Roshani* for December 1953 commented that for millions Vijaya Lakshmi Pandit now personified 'the triumph of the women's movement after over half a century of struggle. . . . It is significant that in an hour of struggle in Asia, one of Asia's daughters should be chosen to become the head of the world assembly of nations'. It was even more remarkable that her election should have the support of the world's three greatest powers—the United States, Russia, and Great Britain—who thus demonstrated 'their awareness of the shifts and changes which have been going on in global politics'.

The United Nations' headquarters—described by its own Information Service as 'a world capital on the East River'—was already one of the most famous modern buildings in New York when Vijaya Lakshmi knew it as President. An example of the new up-ended biscuit-box type of structure, it was soon to have, for better for worse, a striking influence on other buildings in the United States and elsewhere. Its rising shaft of white marble and wide expanse of green-tinted glass overlooked the East River and commanded an extensive view of Manhattan

# United Nations 117

Bridge. One side of the Secretariat's top (38th) floor provided a remarkable panorama of skyscrapers, contrasting with the more human outlook from the side above the East River with its mass of haphazard buildings varied by advertisement hoardings.

Unlike most New York architects, the planners who began their work in 1947 devoted three-quarters of their 18-acre site to grass, trees, shrubs, and gardens. These contained two thousand prize-winning rose bushes, flowering cherries and fruit trees, in addition to a decorative group of hawthorn, sweet gum, pin oaks and honey locust trees. Ilex, myrtle, wisteria and rambler roses adorned the macadam walks. One section of the garden between the central building and the river was much loved by Eleanor Roosevelt, who often sat there. A garden seat in her memory was later placed on the spot.

The General Assembly building, facing a landscaped plaza to the north, was a sloping double concave-shaped structure topped with a shallow dome. A great screen, shagreen in colour to accord with the green carpet beneath the siena-shaded wood of the furniture, dominated the huge auditorium. The United Nations emblem, a symbolic map of the world encircled by an olive branch, adorned the wall above the dais. On each of the side walls, abstract murals by the French artist, Fernand Leger, added to the impression of extreme modernity aimed at by the whole enormous creation. Its architects seemed determined at all costs to avoid any comparison with the abortive buildings in Geneva constructed just before the Second World War for the Secretariat of the League of Nations.

Beneath the vast dome studded with starlight reflectors Vijaya Lakshmi Pandit sat for most of the autumn of 1953, significantly elevated above the great gathering as though she and her companions occupied a detached ornamental shelf floating in the empyrean. The Assembly had been opened that year by Lester Pearson, who spoke briefly in accordance with the now recognized convention that the retiring President should make the first speech. He referred to the previous session (which had lasted until August 28th) as 'the Korean Assembly', and spoke of the heavy burdens imposed on members of national delegations and the Secretariat.

'From the Korean experience we have, I hope, learned some lessons. One is that collective action against aggression can work, even when that action is incomplete in organization, support and participation.'

At the first session Vijaya Lakshmi spoke of the new atmosphere of hope in which they met, but warned the delegates that the Assembly had still to consider other great dangers threatening peace. The chief of

118 *Envoy Extraordinary*

these, as she saw them, were the legitimate urges of rising nationalism, the questions raised by racial friction, and the problems of poverty and want which involved the recognition that 'prosperity and contentment cannot be achieved in compartments'.

As one or another of these dangers arose for discussion during the autumn, she had to adjudicate in the continual Cold War duels between the Soviet delegates Vishinsky and Malik on the one hand, and the American representatives Dulles and Lodge on the other. Early in the session the Soviet speeches ran to great length; Vishinsky's opening address occupied ten and a half double-column pages of the Assembly's official records, an example of verbosity which made it impossible for any other business apart from a short speech by the Liberian delegate to be done that morning. The President was constantly obliged to interrupt the Russian speakers, who appeared indifferent to rules of procedure, but for most of New York's hot September days she listened patiently.

She soon absorbed the detailed technical knowledge required of a United Nations President, and learned to recognize the subleties lying beneath apparently innocuous motions and proposals. Later, however, in England, when she was asked by a reporter what she regarded as the most valuable work outside strictly political discussions done by the Assembly during the year of her Presidency, she did not comment on her own attempts to reconcile conflicting ideologies. These, she said, were less of a threat to peace than the division of the world between privileged and under-privileged nations.

'War and conflicts will continue until that gap is filled. This is what the United Nations specialized agencies are trying to do through raising standards, education, better concepts of democracy, technical skills.'

At the 187th dinner meeting of the Economic Club of New York at the Astor Hotel on November 18, 1953, she had already told the Western Allies that they had largely themselves to blame for the menace of Asian Communism during the recent war. The test of any ideology in Asia, she explained, was not its basic excellence or philosophy, but whether it could become a liberating force 'within the context of the Asian situation'.

Just before the session ended on December 9, 1953, General Eisenhower, elected American President in November 1952, addressed the Assembly, and commented that never before in history had so much hope for so many people been gathered within a single organization. The proceedings closed with a graceful complimentary address to the

## United Nations

President from Andrei Vishinsky, and a short paean of praise from the Indian delegation. Whatever the private feelings of its leader, Krishna Menon, he concluded with a tribute which was a small masterpiece of tact and appreciation.

'Today we are a proud people and a proud delegation. I am sure that in no part of the world more than in India will there be the feeling that we have done a signal service to the United Nations by allowing your name to be put forward for election as its President... We are extremely grateful to you, Madam President, and we are very proud of you.'

Three days later Vijaya Lakshmi left for India. Before her, after a short respite, lay six months of travel in Asia and Europe at the invitation of member nations whose delegations she had met in New York. She began these journeys in March with visits to Madras and Colombo, where the Prime Ministers of India, Pakistan, Burma, Ceylon and Indonesia were to meet in conference from April 28th to May 2nd. Here she stayed with the Prime Minister of Ceylon, and at a great public meeting she made a strong appeal for 'the creation of a climate in which peace can thrive'. She added that 'the West is in a peculiar psychosis of fear; we in India have suffered in a different way'. The first task, she said, was the creation of a new pattern of living, and the conquest of such enemies as ill-health, poverty and repression.

She returned briefly to India for a reception by the civic institutions of Jamnagar and for an address at Lucknow, where scientists of Uttar Pradesh had supported a statement by Jawaharlal Nehru on recent nuclear explosions which appealed for a ban on the manufacture and use of the H-bomb. Almost simultaneously Vijaya Lakshmi, as President of the newly-formed Indian Section of the Women's International League for Peace and Freedom, published on April 13th a similar appeal signed by herself and all the women Members of India's Parliament.

'We have been greatly distressed by the recent Hydrogen Bomb explosions in the Pacific.

'Along with thinking people everywhere we believe that the danger to civilization is greater today than at any previous time and the growing fear in men's hearts is likely to result in the total collapse of those values of faith and morality without which humanity will become a ship without compass or star to guide its course through a stormy sea ...

'The alternative to fear is hope, based on wise and courageous

120 *Envoy Extraordinary*

leadership which, recognizing differences, continues the patient search for a common pattern in which the diverse world society may live together in security and peace.

'We appeal to the statesmen of all nations to give such leadership to the world in this hour of peril.'

In June Vijaya Lakshmi made an eight-day visit to Jugoslavia and was received by President Tito at his summer residence on Brioni Island in the North Adriatic. Various official luncheons and receptions ended with a Press Conference in Zagreb. Here, as so often, she was a path-finder, for visits between Mr Nehru and President Tito were exchanged in December 1954 and June 1955.

She left Jugoslavia for England by way of Switzerland, where the Indian Ambassador Mr Y. D. Gundevia met her at Zürich airport. In London Mr Selwyn Lloyd and India's Acting High Commissioner, Mr M. J. Desai, welcomed her as a State guest. She was received by the Queen at Buckingham Palace and at Chartwell by Sir Winston Churchill, then reaching the end of his second period as Prime Minister.

In a final broadcast from London she emphasized once more the urgent need to reduce the gap between privileged and under-privileged nations. Unless this were narrowed, she thought, it would be difficult to avoid war.

During that year India withdrew her diplomatic mission to South Africa at South Africa's own request, leaving contacts to be maintained between the respective High Commissions in London. South Africa's official reasons were the absence in Cape Town of an Indian High Commissioner and the operation of trade sanctions against the Union since 1948. These steps, long-range consequences of India's frustration which Vijaya Lakshmi had first brought before the United Nations in 1946, were respectively protests against the Asiatic Land Tenure Bill, and against the Group Areas Act which finally achieved the segregation in South Africa of people of Indian descent. Eighteen years after her initial protest, in accordance with a Resolution adopted by the 17th Session of the United Nations, India banned all South African ships and planes from visiting Indian sea and airports.

In London, at a reception given by the Women's Council on July 9, 1954, Vijaya Lakshmi had paid a tribute to her old friend Agatha Harrison, one of those whose support 'had made the achievement of Indian independence possible'. Agatha's sudden death at Geneva on May 10th that year had been one of those heavy blows which seemed

## United Nations 121

to fall on her when her responsibilities were making maximum demands on her energies and powers of concentration. Later, in a small volume of reminiscences published by the Women's International League for Peace and Freedom, she wrote of Agatha that 'for her friends—and they are scattered all over the globe—the world has suddenly become a very empty place'. And she recalled their last meeting at New York's Idlewild Airport.

'As we said good-bye she held my hand tightly in both her own and I shall never forget her parting words, which have now acquired an added significance—"My friend," she said, "my dear friend—you will not give up—you will go on because our prayers are with you." I see her now waving as my plane rose into the air.'

That winter, and for the next seven years, Agatha Harrison's prophecy that Vijaya Lakshmi would 'go on and not give up' was to be fulfilled by the sternest test and heaviest responsibility that she would be called on to face. On September 9th she met Mr Harold Macmillan, Britain's Foreign Secretary since Sir Anthony Eden had taken Winston Churchill's place as Premier, and expressed to him India's concern for the free functioning of the Armistice Supervisory Commission in Vietnam. Three months later, the World Press announced her own appointment as India's High Commissioner to the United Kingdom.

CHAPTER 10

# The Conquest of Britain

VIJAYA LAKSHMI PANDIT's period of nearly seven years as Indian High Commissioner in Britain was divided, as by a steep watershed, by the events of 1956 which included the Suez crisis and the Hungarian revolt. Until that turbulent year, with its reminiscences of nineteenth-century politics, she moved in relatively calm waters, and returned to them, though not immediately, after the storm created by the two crises had subsided.

During her opening months, the prospect looked fair enough. Tension continued between the two great power-blocs in East and West, but it was generally agreed that the danger of a global war had receded, and India received much appreciation for her part in the Armistice agreements which had ended the wars in Korea and Indo-China. Her foreign policy continued to be based on two major principles of co-existence: non-interference in the affairs of other countries, and the right of each country to carve out its destiny unhindered.[1]

At the Bandung Conference of twenty-nine Asian and African States organized by the five Colombo Powers in April 1955, the new Asia and Africa visibly emerged into world affairs. At the request of the Geneva Conference of 1954, India had accepted the Chairmanship of the three Commissions for Vietnam, Laos and Cambodia, charged with the task of ending the hostilities in the peninsula which had raged continuously since the end of the Second World War. India's diplomatic relations with China, established only a few weeks after the inauguration of the People's Republic, had been strengthened by Jawaharlal Nehru's visit in 1954 which followed Vijaya Lakshmi's tour of 1952. At the Tenth (1955) Assembly of the United Nations the Indian delegation, led by Krishna Menon, supported the Russian Resolution for the admission of China. Though tension in Formosa

[1] An exception was South Africa, where the welfare of resident Indians was seriously jeopardized by the Union's *apartheid* policies.

## The Conquest of Britain 123

cast its shadow over the Commonwealth Prime Ministers' Conference in February, the approaching completion of India's First Five-Year Plan added its element of confidence to Vijaya Lakshmi's new appointment.

Her period as High Commissioner both symbolized and typified the changed relationship between India and Britain which had followed Independence. From the time that India became free, Vijaya Lakshmi had always insisted, like her brother, that it was not the British people but the colonial system that she and her country had opposed.

'Our hostility during the last 200 years,' Jawaharlal had said in the Constituent Assembly on March 8, 1949, 'was mainly directed towards the dominating power here, and because of India's independence that hostility has largely vanished though it may survive in some people's minds. So we approach the whole world on a friendly basis.'

At first Vijaya Lakshmi's main task appeared to be that of creating a more enlightened understanding of India in Britain. She hoped also to project her own interpretation of the Commonwealth, which she saw as a bold experiment in co-existence and inter-racial understanding.

When Ludovic Kennedy interviewed her on television shortly before her mission ended, he expressed surprise at her attitude of tolerance after all that she and her family had suffered at British hands. But she insisted that a special bond of sympathy existed between the two peoples. 'Even at the height of British imperialism,' she said in an address to the Royal Central Asian Society in 1961, 'there were elements in Britain whose liberal ideas kept public opinion informed and ultimately influenced Government policies.'

By that time she knew that this instinctive understanding had become the basis for a mature relationship which had been strengthened rather than weakened by the period of strain that she had shared with the British people in 1956–57. She had replaced the old traditional images of British India with the image of a re-born country ready to share in new varieties of co-operation.

When her daughter Nayantara Sahgal stayed in London, she found that the 'damned British' had faded into half-forgotten bogeys of her early years, about as close to reality as the inimical giants of Grimm's *Fairy Tales*. Now, during her visits to her mother, she discovered that a nation of real, reasonable, just and kindly people—even if a trifle lethargic and implacably endowed with common sense—had replaced the menacing hobgoblins of childhood.

On December 19, 1954, Vijaya Lakshmi arrived in London by air to start her intimidating assignment. Though Press photographs showed

124 *Envoy Extraordinary*

that she wore a fur coat over her dark sari to present her credentials to the Queen, and came back to India House in the Royal State coach, the contrast between India's climate and the cheerless English winter at first sent her to bed with a sharp attack of influenza. But she recovered in time to be At Home to all Indian nationals living in London on the anniversary of Republic Day, January 26, 1955, and the previous day to meet her brother on his arrival to attend the Commonwealth Prime Ministers' Conference and be photographed with him on the steps of the Residency.

This ornate mansion stood in a long, impressive, tree-shaded road, running up the western boundary of Kensington Palace from Kensington High Street to the less aristocratic Notting Hill High Street beyond the summit of Campden Hill. Though officially named Kensington Palace Gardens, it was popularly known as 'Millionaires' Row' because its large dwellings had been the homes of several American and other millionaires earlier in the century. Its purchase for the new Indian mission in London had been, strangely enough, the acquisition of India's first High Commissioner, Krishna Menon.

This passionate controversial figure had converted into unaccustomed splendour the saturnine personal frugality inherited from his long struggle to make a living as a lawyer in student lodgings. So far as his British acquaintances could judge he lived entirely on tea—to which Tara in her book *From Fear Set Free* added the slightly more substantial diet of grilled tomatoes. He continued to live in his back room at India House, yet he bought the palatial Kensington mansion and equipped it with costly chandeliers though he neither lived in it nor let it. For him—like India House in Aldwych, where he added one new department after another and increased the secretarial staff from 600 to 1,500—it was presumably a status-symbol of India's changed position in the international community.

Menon's successor, Mr B. G. Kher, occupied one suite in 9 Kensington Palace Gardens and closed the rest. As a former Premier of Bombay he was no doubt accustomed to living economically in that externally prosperous city with its vast hinterland of slums and shacks, and being a bachelor had no particular use for a hall lavishly hung with mirrors, an Adam fire-place in the main reception-room, Marie Antoinette furniture, and hall tapestries imported from a French château on the Loire.

Vijaya Lakshmi Pandit, having by chance become responsible for this costly white elephant, knew exactly how to use it. For nearly seven years her receptions and dinner parties became famous, as also, when

# The Conquest of Britain 125

the English weather permitted, her garden parties on the smooth rose-decorated lawn, with a similar lawn at the Embassy next door, and the green stretch of Kensington Gardens beyond. It was true that the bombs of the war-time blitz, no more respectful of millionaires than of humble workers, had severely damaged an adjoining mansion, but in summer the trees concealed this typically uncleared and ugly ruin. The High Commissioner's Persian miniatures and her own collection of jade added an Indian atmosphere which competed successfully, without exactly clashing, with the French adornments.

The first problem was that of providing an adequate staff. Apart from Vijaya Lakshmi's own Indian cook Buddhi, the Residency was run for a time by students of diverse nationalities working their way through college. As they did not regard preparing trays and arranging flowers as part of their duties, Vijaya Lakshmi added these minor 'chores' to choosing menus and keeping household accounts. After fulfilling with resolute dignity the function of Ambassador at India House, she also became the Ambassador's wife on returning to the Residency. Nayantara quotes one heartfelt comment: 'Unfortunately for me there's never been a staff here before, or, properly speaking, an Ambassador.' She nevertheless appeared at her numerous At Homes to meet crowds of guests in a handsome sari which always seemed to have been newly pressed, without a hair out of place on her elegant silver-grey head.[1] Finally, two well-trained Indian bearers arrived from home to solve, as in Moscow, her domestic problem.

In January 1955, with the Indian Prime Minister's arrival, she began the task of travelling, negotiating, receiving innumerable visitors, and addressing significant and varied audiences all over the country, which was to occupy her almost without a break for the next six and a half years. Whether the audiences were composed of University teachers and students, bankers, schools, business men, or the vast unspecified listeners to the Brains' Trust, she seemed equally at home with them all. No other woman in the world, with the probable exception of Eleanor Roosevelt, with whom she once made a brief joint tour, so keenly enjoyed this life of continuous travelling and speaking.

At her first official dinner, given by the Indian Social Club which was the leading Indian organization in the United Kingdom, her fellow

---

[1] Once, owing to a mistake in a diary entry, my husband and I arrived at one of her At Homes half an hour before the time fixed. Within minutes she was receiving us, reinforced by an appropriate sprinkling of Embassy officials, without a trace of the exasperation which all busy people feel when their guests arrive too soon.

V.B.

126 *Envoy Extraordinary*

guests included the Soviet Ambassador, Jacob Malik, with whom she had crossed swords at the United Nations. In replying to the toast, she told her Indian audience that they had perhaps greater responsibilities in Britain than if they were living in India.

'You and I together must represent the real India, the new young India, the India full of aspirations which is moving into wider and wider responsibilities and, in co-operation with other nations, is trying to build a stable, peaceful world.'

Between January 1955 and the end of the year, her numerous audiences included the Indian Chamber of Commerce; the Association of Business and Professional Women at the Connaught Rooms, where 350 would-be guests who wanted to join the audience of 750 were unable to get in; the annual dinner at University College, London; the annual service of the World Congress of Faiths at Kingsway Hall; the tenth Birthday Dinner of the United Nations Association at the Guildhall; the students of fifty nations at Loughborough College; a luncheon at the Royal Empire (later Commonwealth) Society, where she spoke on 'India's Place in the Modern World'; several Scottish audiences, including the Edinburgh branch of the English-speaking Union, during a ten days' visit to Scotland in August; the first Woman of the Year Luncheon in September; and a luncheon at the Savoy Hotel for Lord Home, then Secretary of State for Commonwealth Affairs, on his return from visiting Commonwealth countries.

One important engagement involved a luncheon with the Manchester Chamber of Commerce, followed by four other addresses to Manchester organizations before she caught the midnight train back to London. This visit followed representations by the Cotton Board, whose Chairman, Sir Raymond Streat, mentioned the serious handicap to Lancashire textiles imposed by the advantageous raw cotton prices for the Indian industry, and asked that something 'other than arithmetic' should create an understanding, including a possible 'ceiling' on Indian exports to the United Kingdom, between the two branches of the trade.

At a visit to Wales in October Vijaya Lakshmi spoke six times in two days, though she was scheduled only for three engagements. These included an address on 'India's Foreign Policy' organized by the Welsh Council of the United Nations, at which the eighty-one-year-old Mayor of Cardiff said he had never seen Wood Street Church, where the meeting took place, so full since his early twenties. When she finished her speech, the audience of over 4,000 people stood up and clapped her for five minutes.

## The Conquest of Britain 127

Between these stimulating occasions she managed to visit Dublin in March 1955, to present her credentials to the President of Eire, Mr Sean T. O'Ceallaigh, as 'India's Ambassador Extraordinary and Plenipotentiary to the Republic of Ireland'. She was the first woman Ambassador to Dublin since Eire became a republic in 1949. Hitherto relationships with India had been handled from London, but now she managed to cross the Irish Sea periodically as diplomatic business required. Her first important mission was to prepare for a trade agreement; Eire wanted tea from India in return for agricultural and light industrial machinery, pottery and hides.

Her mind, she said as she presented her credentials, was full of memories 'of the heroic past of this beautiful land which has so greatly influenced my own generation in India—and even though we walked by different roads to reach the goal of freedom, the courage and sacrifice of Ireland's leaders was an inspiration in our struggle'.

Just after her return to London an abortive attempt was made in India on her brother's life, causing her a short period of acute anxiety.

'It was very sweet of you to wire and write to me,' she wrote to the author. 'I had a bad morning after the news came as I could not contact India and was not sure how authentic the Press report was. However, all seems well and I am deeply thankful.'

During her first eighteen months she received three Honorary Degrees as Doctor of Laws, two from Leeds University and the University of Wales in 1956, and one on November 15, 1955, from London University at the personal desire of the Queen Mother, who was installed as Chancellor that year. In presenting Vijaya Lakshmi the Public Orator, Sir Ifor Evans, described her work as High Commissioner as a symbol of the forgiveness and reconciliation which united India and Britain after Independence. The foundations of this were largely laid by four people—Sir Stafford Cripps, Lord Pethick-Lawrence, and Lord and Lady Mountbatten. He added: 'Our political behaviour, here in England, can claim to have at least one endearing quality. We do not allow arguments, whether present or past, to cool the warmth of our friendship and affection for those who may once have counted us their adversaries.'

These events, and some significant speaking engagements in the first half of 1956, which included a response to Republic Day speeches by Lord Home and Hugh Gaitskell at the Indian Journalists' Anniversary Dinner, an important address in Manchester to the Royal Institute of International Affairs, and a speech at the annual summer rally of Women's Institutes at the Albert Hall, took place against the

128    *Envoy Extraordinary*

changing background of foreign affairs in both Britain and India which for her had to take precedence over all else.

In April 1955 a change of Government had occurred at Westminster, when Sir Anthony Eden replaced Sir Winston Churchill as Premier. Ten months later her long-standing rival, Krishna Menon, became a Cabinet Minister in India. In May 1956 she received India's Vice-President, Sir Sarvepalli Radhakrishnan, and gave a reception for him in Kensington Palace Gardens. In June followed her brother's official visit for the Commonwealth Prime Ministers' Conference; she arranged a garden party for him at the Residency, and on July 2nd accompanied him on a visit to Ireland.

That year 1956 had seen the completion of India's First Five-Year Plan. Several projects undertaken through the Colombo Plan included an agreement between India and Canada in April to set up a high-powered atomic reactor in India for the peaceful uses of atomic energy. This was eventually established at Trombay, near Bombay.

1956 was also the 'Year of the Buddha', in which all Asia celebrated the 2,500th anniversary of the prophet's 'Parmirvana', and Buddhist pilgrims from many lands included a delegation from the United Kingdom.

On May 28th, as the long-term results of friendly negotiations, came the welcome Treaty which marked the formal end of French colonial rule in Indian enclaves, and Karikal, Pondicherry, Mahe, and Yanain were ceded to India under arrangements that guaranteed the preservation of the French language and culture. This civilized arrangement led to a pronouncement on Portuguese-held Goa by Jawaharlal Nehru, who said that India would not tolerate 'the continuance of fifteenth-century colonialism on Indian soil', though she intended to handle this problem peacefully also, and to persuade Portugal to follow the example of France. Finally, three agreements were signed in May providing for financial aid amounting to $736,682,000 from the United States for India's development projects.

Watching these reassuring events from afar, and stimulated as always by her brother's visit, Vijaya Lakshmi felt that 1956 had given her a rewarding spring and summer. But by the end of July an ominous shadow had suddenly descended across the bright international scene.

On July 26th President Nasser announced to the world in a speech at Alexandria that the nationalization of the Suez Canal had been effected. The control of the Canal Company's offices at Port Said, Ismailia, Suez and Cairo would be taken over by the State, which

# The Conquest of Britain 129

would pay compensation, and the management of the Canal traffic entrusted to an independent authority with its own budget and full powers, which left it free from Government regulations.

An international uproar followed this declaration, which aroused fears and passions among the users of the Canal. India, which was one of them, felt that since the Canal was in Egypt and an integral part of it, Egypt's sovereignty was beyond question. She had a close affinity with Egypt and with the Arab nations which were co-members of the Bandung Conference, and had always emphasized the evil effects of various Middle Eastern pacts and military alliances by which the Great Powers sought to protect their interests.

These, she thought, caused tensions (such as the divisions in the Arab League) without adding to security—an assessment in which Egypt concurred. Personal visits had been exchanged between Jawaharlal Nehru and President Nasser, and on April 6, 1955, a treaty of friendship between India and Egypt had been signed in Cairo. But India also had intimate relations with Britain and other Western States to add to her problems. Above all, she had a passionate interest in averting a conflict of which the results could not be foreseen.

'I have no desire to add to the passions aroused,' Jawaharlal stated in the Lok Sabha on August 8, 1956, 'but I would fail in my duty to this House and the country, and even to all the parties involved in this crisis, and not least of all Britain and France, if I do not say that threats to settle this dispute or to enforce their views in this matter by display or use of force is the wrong way. It does not belong to this age and it is not dictated by reason.'

On August 16th the British Government summoned a Conference of twenty-two nations to discuss the Suez crisis at London's Lancaster House. India sent a strong delegation, led by Krishna Menon, now Minister without Portfolio, who broke his journey in Cairo for talks with President Nasser. Vijaya Lakshmi Pandit joined this delegation as soon as it arrived. On August 6th, in search of clarification, she had discussed the crisis with Britain's Foreign Secretary, Mr Selwyn Lloyd.

At the Conference, in a sincere endeavour to find a solution, Krishna Menon put forward a plan of which the operative section was an item providing for 'the association of international user-interests with Egyptian co-operation for the Suez Canal'. India believed that Menon's proposals, which clearly recognized the sovereign rights of Egypt, would have been an effective alternative to the Dulles Plan, which sought to impose a solution upon Egypt by setting up an International

130                    *Envoy Extraordinary*

Board for the administration and operation of the Canal. But India
failed to get the support of the Western Powers, and eventually, with
the Soviet Union, Indonesia, and Ceylon, disassociated herself from the
eighteen-nation proposals based on the Dulles Plan.

Meanwhile Vijaya Lakshmi's own special duties as Indian High
Commissioner had to continue. On September 6th she visited Edinburgh to attend the world *première* of the Indian ballet, 'The Legend
of the Taj Mahal', by Ram Gopal and his troupe; to dine with the Lord
Provost Sir John G. Banks, and to entertain a hundred Indian students
who were her guests at the Caledonian Hotel. For this festival tea she
had Indian sweets and savouries flown from London. She followed these
engagements by a goodwill visit to Birmingham which included a
reception for the civic heads of seven Midland towns and a visit to
Woodbrooke, the Quaker centre at Selly Oak.

On October 10th she flew to India for a short holiday, combined
with consultations on the international crisis. Pressed by reporters for
an opinion on Suez, she replied diplomatically that both Britain and
India wanted a peaceful solution. But at the end of the month came a
series of events raising problems as difficult as those of the Korean War,
which did not exactly subscribe to the Buddha's ideal of love, tolerance
and compassion, and made a peaceful solution seem farther away than
ever.

Vijaya Lakshmi was still in India on November 3rd when she saw a
startling newspaper headline, 'India shocked by Anglo-French Action
in Egypt', and heard her brother comment: 'In all my experience of
foreign affairs I have come across no grosser case of naked aggression
than what England and France are trying to do.' On November 16th,
a day after her return to London, he related to the Lok Sabha in Delhi
the sequence of dismaying events. Instead of supporting a proposal by
the Security Council that Egypt, Britain and France should meet to
discuss the Suez dispute, Israel had launched a sudden, premeditated
attack on Egypt on October 29th and large concentrations of Israeli
troops had penetrated deeply into Egyptian territory.

The next day the British and French Governments sent to Egypt
and Israel an ultimatum which said that if they did not stop fighting
and withdraw their forces ten miles from either side of the Suez Canal,
British and French troops would intervene. Soon after the ultimatum
expired on October 31st, British and French troops began to bombard
airfields in Cairo and elsewhere in Egypt. A few days later came the
landing of airborne troops in Port Said, followed by heavy fighting.

The outcry which followed this reversion to the nineteenth-century

# The Conquest of Britain 131

methods by which Great Powers sought to impose their will upon weaker countries was as loud in Britain as anywhere else. From the windows of India House, Vijaya Lakshmi could see the crowds hurrying to Trafalgar Square for a unique protest meeting, addressed by Aneurin Bevan, Edith Summerskill, and other Labour and Liberal politicians to the accompaniment of smoke bombs and shouts of 'Eden must go!' which extended into the surrounding streets and amounted to an estimated audience of 20,000. Similar American reactions were expressed in forthright words which did not spare the responsible British Government. Almost simultaneously arose the crisis created on October 23rd by the Hungarian revolt against Soviet domination. The tragedies of Suez and Hungary were not related except that the repercussions of each affected the other, and added to the danger created by international tension.

'The fact is,' unequivocally said Jawaharlal Nehru in a debate on Foreign Affairs on November 19, 1956, 'that each group is attempting to lay stress on what has happened in the other place, so as to hide its own misdemeanour.'

India's view that what mattered in Hungary was not an outburst of indignation, but the end of internal fighting and bloodshed, was largely misunderstood in the West. In New York Krishna Menon had to explain to the United Nations Assembly that 'we are not neutral where human freedom is concerned', but 'we are against the intervention of any government, any outside authority, with the affairs of States from whatever quarter it may come or whatsoever form it may take'. In January 1957, during a New Year visit to Ireland, Vijaya Lakshmi referred in a broadcast from Radio Eireann to the hundred letters she had received from Irish correspondents questioning India's sincerity with regard to Hungary.

'India's attempt,' she explained, 'has been to try and build a bridge between areas of conflict. The Indian Government wish to make a real contribution to the basic issue, which is the withdrawal of Soviet troops and the right of the Hungarian people to freedom. Merely joining in a chorus of condemnation would not have been of much assistance.'

With relief she spoke of Ireland's present freedom from the turbulence once so fully experienced. 'There is some strange quality in this Emerald Island which is very soothing and those who come here from less restful places are tempted to relax and seek escape from the harassments and worries which have become our common lot. But escape is not easy—how can one escape from one's thoughts?'

## 132 Envoy Extraordinary

The series of international crises had its political consequences for Britain. Early in January 1957 came another change of Prime Minister, when Anthony Eden—already a sick man before he began his harassing Premiership—gave way to Harold Macmillan. In February came India's second General Election, in which the passing of the Hindu Code legislation keenly affected the women's votes.

On November 1, 1956, the Hindu Succession Bill had become an Act, and this put the climax to a series of small measures dealing with Marriage, Guardianship, Minority, and Adoption. Vijaya Lakshmi, whose own life would have been beneficially affected by this legislation had it come thirteen years earlier, was now able to tell her audiences that Hindu women's rights to property were about the best such rights for women anywhere in the world. The 1951 Census had revealed that 5 million Indian women were now self-supporting. At the Election twenty-seven women candidates were elected to the Lok Sabha (Lower or People's House), and twenty-three to the Upper House, Rajya Sabha. For the State Assemblies 342 women had stood, and 195 were elected. Temporarily these events had turned Vijaya Lakshmi's thoughts from diplomacy to active politics. Among the Congress candidates her brother, with a lead of 193,000 votes over his three rivals, and Maulana Azad had topped the poll, which gave Congress an absolute majority of seats.

It was perhaps a pleasant change on February 23rd for Vijaya Lakshmi to address the Liverpool Soroptimists at their thirtieth anniversary dinner on 'The Rôle of Women in the Modern World', though no one could have said that the events of the preceding twelve months had made life easier for either men or women in public life. In spite of never looking at politics from what the Press calls 'the women's angle', she had every reason for thinking that the contribution of women might have a healing effect on the human society which men had so often shattered with their hatreds and rages.

'I do believe,' she said, 'that women have certain qualities which are greatly required today. These qualities are tolerance, patience, perseverance, which have developed as a result of being suppressed for a period. At this delicate period of world history these qualities can be well used to help turn the balance from suspicion and hatred into trust and love.'

As the passions roused by the Suez and Hungarian crises slowly faded, the London atmosphere returned to the relative peace of her first twelve months, with routine business periodically interrupted by travels and speeches. She visited Northern Ireland in April 1957, and

## The Conquest of Britain 133

spoke to a meeting of the Belfast English-speaking Union on the recent tensions between India and Britain over both Suez and Kashmir. Many Indians believed that British support for Pakistan in the debate on Kashmir in the Security Council earlier in the year had been a form of retaliation for India's attitude on Suez. In the hope of restoring Indo-British relations to rational normality, Vijaya Lakshmi spent two weeks in Delhi after her journey to Belfast.

She came back in time to join Bertrand Russell on the Brains' Trust which celebrated his eighty-fifth birthday on May 19th, and a month later to welcome her brother at the Commonwealth Prime Ministers' Conference which testified that the crisis of confidence which had undermined Commonwealth relations for the past twelve months had been surmounted. In November rumours that India was considering a withdrawal from the Commonwealth had caused great perturbation to Lord Pethick-Lawrence, the veteran former Secretary of State for India. Vijaya Lakshmi was now able to reassure him that the Indian Government did not propose to desert those British people who had protested against the 'disgrace' of the Suez crisis.

'It has been heartening for us in India,' she wrote to him, 'to realize that the UK Government's action in Egypt did not have the support of a large number of people of all groups in this country. I think my brother has made it clear that India would not wish to leave the Commonwealth and that she believes that our continuing membership is of benefit not only to ourselves but to the United Kingdom.'

In July Vijaya Lakshmi accompanied Jawaharlal on his first visit to Holland and was photographed with Queen Juliana at the Soestdijk Palace. Her brother returned to India to celebrate ten years of Independence on August 15th. Two days earlier the Mahatma's youngest son Devadas, the Managing Editor of the *Hindustan Times,* had died at the age of fifty-six, and removed from the Nehru family circle one more friend who had been virtually a member of it—'linked to us by ties which are closer than blood'.

At the end of August the new Premier announced that he and his wife would travel to India in January 1958; he would be the first British Prime Minister to make such a visit on equal terms. This gesture of reconciliation further re-established Indo-British relations, though the dire events of the past twelve months had exhausted Vijaya Lakshmi more than she then realized. On November 9th she flew to San Francisco to address the closing plenary session of the Sixth National Conference of the US National Commissions for UNESCO, and told 1,500 distinguished delegates from thirty-nine countries that the

# 134 *Envoy Extraordinary*

world could not remain indefinitely 'half ox-cart and half Cadillac . . . this imbalance is a far greater danger than the deadliest weapon of destruction.'

Referring to America's well-remembered support for India's national struggle, she said that she hoped for ultimate mutual understanding between the United States and the restless nations of new Asia, but added frankly:

'I would like to remind you how sensitive we still are to any form of discrimination on ground of race or colour. For this reason the smallest item of news from Asia or Africa which relates to discrimination often makes a disproportionate impact on the African mind. The question of racial prejudice undoubtedly remains one of the chief barriers between our world and yours.'

On January 8th Vijaya Lakshmi accompanied Harold Macmillan and his wife, Lady Dorothy, to India for their official visit. They had both dined with her at the Residency a month earlier, and now she heard her brother's welcome to him at a banquet in Dehi on January 9th. Mr Nehru spoke especially of the manner in which the changed relations between Britain and India had been brought about.

'The manner is not only unique, but strangely dramatic, which after these long years of conflict, almost as if by a magic wand, put an end to that spirit of conflict, and led to a desire to co-operate in spite of very considerable differences in opinion or on our reaction to events. This was not only remarkable in itself, but in some measure, I think, it has set a pattern from which others might profit.'

One country which seemed unlikely to profit by that particular transformation was Ghana, but when Vijaya Lakshmi went there for three days in April 1958 and stayed at the Christiansborg Castle (later Government House) as the guest of the Prime Minister, Kwame Nkrumah, she was almost overwhelmend by the number of her engagements. After half a dozen functions in Accra, she visited Kumasi, Ghana's 'Garden City', and was greeted by joyous shouts of 'Freedom, Nehru's sister!' from men and women in gorgeous garments who included Zongo Muslims on horseback.

She expressed surprise at the exuberance of this traditional welcome before going on to India for a short holiday. As always it was not a complete holiday; at Srinagar on May 19th she opened the Kashmir Spring Festival at a mass youth rally where 25,000 people were present

## The Conquest of Britain 135

to enjoy the flowers, balloons, and multi-coloured festoons which adorned the beautiful lofty city.

In June she returned to London after an absence of nearly two months, to find her appointment recorded as the first Indian Ambassador to Madrid. Spain and India had decided in May 1956 to establish diplomatic relations at Embassy level, and now made her the first woman, and probably the first diplomat, to hold three ambassadorships simultaneously She visited Madrid to present her credentials on October 30, 1957, and was officially photographed with General Franco. In November came yet another foreign visit, when she was invited to Germany to receive the Dorothy Schlozer Medal, which commemorated the first woman to take the degree of Doctor of Philosophy at the University of Göttingen in 1787. Vijaya Lakshmi had been chosen as the first recipient of this medal, said the Rector of the University, because she was 'one of the strongest symbols of the fundamentally changed position of women in modern society'.

Like 1958, the year 1959 proved to be a normal diplomatic year without an international crisis to interrupt the colourful sequence of speeches and travels. In January she spoke at a Republic Day Dinner with Britain's last Viceroy for India, and said of him: 'I would like to think of Lord Mountbatten as the first Englishman who inaugurated a new era for India.' A year later Edwina Mountbatten, the dauntless and elegant Vicereine who had shared that task with him, died suddenly in North Borneo while on a tour of the East. In a radio tribute Vijaya Lakshmi said she could not believe that such a vital personality had slipped so quietly away. After referring to her old friend's special quality of 'effortless grace', she related the characteristic story of an occasion on which Lady Mountbatten had thrust aside protocol and followed the instincts of her courageous spirit.

'I remember one night when the word came to my brother that the Jamia Milia—the National Muslim College on the outskirts of Delhi—was about to be attacked by a hostile crowd and the situation was said to be full of danger. My brother immediately jumped up and ordered a car to take him to the Jamia. On arrival he found the Vicereine already there, unaccompanied, working with a group of volunteers to calm the excited people. Edwina's actions, so simple in their spontaneity, so statesmanlike in their effect, undoubtedly contributed to the easing of tension.'

On February 2, 1959, Vijaya Lakshmi's niece Indira became President of Congress, but eighteen months later, in September 1960, lost

136     *Envoy Extraordinary*

her husband, Feroze Gandhi. In March 1959, Vijaya Lakshmi paid official visits to Newcastle-upon-Tyne, Liverpool, and Sheffield, and two months later flew to Chicago to speak at a dinner in honour of Eleanor Roosevelt's seventy-fifth birthday. She said that Mrs Roosevelt had come to be regarded in India as 'a symbol of the values by which people live', and recalled that she had first met her in 1945.

'During these fourteen demanding years I have watched her untiring efforts to break the barriers which separate men and nations; I have seen her strive to create an awareness of the need for a common conception of the purposes and destiny of humanity. She has *given* herself to this work. With her it was not a duty to be discharged, or even an act of faith; it was the result of the compelling desire which insists on the complete identification of one's self with what one believes to be right. Because of this she can go on, day after day, not seeking any reward, not minding criticism, knowing that ends are taken care of if the means are right.'

'There is, I think,' she added, 'considerable significance in the fact that an Indian woman has been asked to pay the first tribute this evening.' Referring again to America's long association with India's freedom struggle, she concluded: 'America's stand on India during this period encouraged and strengthened us. The ideals of the American Revolution, so similar to our own, were an inspiration. The Four Freedoms held a hope for us as for many others.'

She remained in the United States for a three weeks' lecture tour, and returned for a series of December engagements which included opening an exhibition of paintings by Sylvia Pankhurst that revealed 'the remarkable talents' of one who had given up a promising career as an artist for the Suffragette movement.

The Spring of 1960 saw the birth of two new Indian States, Maharashtra and Gujerat; with the first of these, an enlargement of the old Bombay Presidency, her future was soon to be linked. A few days later her brother arrived for that year's Commonwealth Prime Ministers' Conference, and they went together to visit Jennie Lee and Aneurin Bevan—who had dropped everything at Vijaya's request to go to India after Suez and resuscitate India's regard for Britain by explaining the Labour Party standpoint—at their Ashridge farm. Aneurin was then convalescent after a severe operation, and the four of them were photographed together. Two months later, following a relapse, he was dead.

In September Vijaya Lakshmi became the President of a joint Indo-British Committee to draw up a programme for the Tagore Centenary

## The Conquest of Britain    137

in 1961. Shortly afterwards she received at India House a portrait of her brother, unveiled by Lord Pethick-Lawrence, to mark Mr Nehru's seventy-first birthday on November 14th.

Before the Tagore Centenary celebrations began the Queen and Prince Philip had visited India, thereby symbolizing the final restoration of cordial Indo-British relations. The High Commissioner went with the Queen, accompanying her on long journeys all over India. For four weeks Vijaya Lakshmi took infinite trouble to make sure, at each centre visited, that the arrangements were efficient.

When the Queen and her husband landed in bright morning sunshine at Delhi airport on January 21, 1961, not only President Prasad and the Cabinet Ministers and Commonwealth High Commissioners greeted them but—probably to their astonishment—thousands of cheering people, who lined the route all the way to the President's house, Rashtrapati Bhawan. Nearly a million spectators, assembled in Delhi to celebrate Republic Day, watched their first drive in an open car and entertained them with folk dances and music.

At the State banquet held for them that evening, Dr Prasad reminded the Queen that it was exactly fifty years since her grandfather, George V, visited Delhi, while Independence was attained under her father. That event had changed the whole aspect of the relationship between the two countries. 'This happy result,' he concluded, 'has been achieved on the one hand by the timely action of the British in parting with power effectively and gracefully and, on the other, by the teachings of Mahatma Gandhi, the philosopher and leader who guided us to this new destiny.'

Vijaya Lakshmi returned to England on March 2nd, and entertained the Queen and Prince Philip to dinner at the Residency on March 28th. She knew that the tour, and the public relations which she had conducted in India, represented a crowning triumph; the Queen, a young woman still under thirty-five, had clearly enjoyed the strenuous journeys and had appreciated, not least, her own unexpected popularity. But for Vijaya Lakshmi, after six years of responsible and often anxious diplomacy, preceded by two other important missions and her own conspicuous rôle at the United Nations, the cost had been heavy.

The portrait of her presented to her brother in March, which showed her in an attractive white dress looking as comely as ever, betrayed no trace of her fatigue.[1] But her health was definitely failing when she made one of the most successful speeches she ever delivered in England at Foyle's farewell luncheon in her honour on April 19, 1961, when

[1] See frontispiece.

138 *Envoy Extraordinary*

Lord Morrison of Lambeth took the Chair and Lord Attlee was a guest. By a significant coincidence the centenary celebrations for her father, Motilal Nehru, began that month at Agra, to be followed in May by similar functions at Allahabad.

'As I have sat here in the past,' Vijaya Lakshmi said at the Dorchester Hotel to her hostess, Christina Foyle, 'I have always been thinking how nice it would be if some day, perhaps, I could be standing at a Foyle Luncheon as the guest of honour.'

She referred to the 'complete harmony and friendship' of the existing relations between Britain and India, 'which would not have been possible had there not always been this difference between our movement for independence and other such movements—that though we disapprove of the system, we never disapproved of the people. There is a Sanscrit saying of which I often think—and I think of it particularly today. It says that the scope of happiness is hampered by the acts and hurts of endless sorrow. Everything has to come to an end, and this happy period of my life—and not only happy but immensely fruitful and enriching for me as a period—is drawing to a close; and I think it right that it should, because there comes a time in one's life when one is interpreting the country to which one is accredited with greater ability than one's own needs, aims and aspirations; and I am afraid I have just reached the border line. If I were to stay on here in an official capacity for very much longer I would be your Ambassador instead of being the Indian Ambassador, so I hasten home before any tragedy befalls my reputation!'

But she was not yet able to go home. On April 22nd she wrote to the author: 'The doctor has put me to bed for a week as he says I am quite exhausted. I am very annoyed but feel it is wise to be guided by him. I shall therefore have to postpone our little dinner party on the 25th to another day. *Do* forgive me.'

At the beginning of May she was obliged to cancel all her engagements owing to 'continuous indisposition', and to rest for a time at the London Clinic. The Tagore Centenary meeting on May 8th at the Albert Hall, where she was to have presided on her father's own birthday which was also the poet's, was conducted by Reginald Sorensen, MP, in her absence, though she sent a message commenting on Tagore's identification of himself with 'mankind's search for happiness and peace, and his eternal quest for self-realization'.

She recovered sufficiently early in July to travel to Edinburgh and Dublin to add two more University doctorates to the eleven that she had already collected in addition to many other honours and awards.

## The Conquest of Britain    139

The rest of the month went by in a chorus of farewells, amounting to three parties a day, scores of letters from friends both known and unknown, and articles in every leading newspaper. She found these valedictory tributes gratifying but also painful; in the words of a French proverb which she had quoted at Foyle's Luncheon: 'Every parting means dying a little'. On August 14th she relinquished her post, and left for a holiday in Greece on her way back to India.

As High Commissioner her work had fallen into two categories. It had given her ample experience of the small change of negotiation, such as the social contacts and public engagements in which a tactful word or two could change the balance of human relationships, but it had also confronted her with some really tough diplomatic problems which compelled her to explain India's attitude to many who disagreed with it. The Anglo-French attack on Egypt, and the British Government's support of Pakistan's manoeuvres against India at the United Nations after the Suez crisis, had imposed a greater strain on Indo-British relations than any event since India became an independent republic, and not the least part of the strain had fallen on herself. Yet she had never believed that it would overwhelm her.

'I had no difficulties of any sort *vis-à-vis* the British Government or people, even after Suez,' she once told a friend, 'and as far as the public were concerned, they were completely understanding.'

Her skill in handling intransigent questions had already been proved at the United Nations when she came to England, but that had been for a shorter period. In London she stood at the very centre of international problems, which she had discussed with sensitive insight. If she sometimes spoke in clichés, every highbrow critic, like every diplomat, should remember that clichés are what the ordinary person understands. Conversion to a point of view is seldom achieved, at any rate in speeches, by the use of literary language, a fact which explains why so few successful politicians are also effective writers.

In London, too, Vijaya Lakshmi had found that in sixteen years the story of her political life had turned full circle. The once imperialist country that she had gone to America to attack in 1945 had become a beloved second home which she was reluctant to leave after nearly seven years of triumphant diplomacy and a unique personal experience of 'the big world outside the diplomatic corps'—the world of bookshops, theatres, and the English countryside—in which she could mix freely with all varieties of people.

And she herself, as the newspaper headlines which announced her departure implied, had been largely responsible for the change. During

# 140 *Envoy Extraordinary*

her tenure of office she had given a new orientation to Indo-British relationships, and had played an important part in the evolution of the Commonwealth to which those relationships were now the key. 'The Nicest Diplomat of Them All', as the Press described her, had conquered Britain by her skill in human relations, and her persistent emphasis on tolerance and reconciliation.

CHAPTER 11

# Bombay and After

EVEN when Vijaya Lakshmi boarded her aircraft on August 14, 1961, carrying two enormous farewell bouquets, she had not quite finished with Europe. In September a grievous tragedy brought her back to the West, though it was to Sweden, not Britain, that she went. She represented India at the State funeral in Upsala of Dag Hammarskjoeld, the Secretary General of the United Nations, whose life had been ended by an air crash in the Congo during a peace mission to strife-ravaged Africa.

His death was a severe blow to the international causes supported by India. On September 28th Vijaya Lakshmi paid tribute to him at a mammoth meeting organized by the citizens of Stockholm to do honour to his memory. Some of her hearers who had been present in New York at meetings of the United Nations in 1953 recalled the two of them sitting gravely together on the uplifted dais of their spectacular Assembly Hall.

'It is a bitter commentary on the age in which we live,' she said, 'that a man like Dag should have had to die in an effort to end strife and restore harmony. We do not need to grieve for Dag, but let us bow our heads in shame at the continuing conflict in the world that demanded sacrifice of Dag's valuable life. Let us deplore greed and hatred and exploitation which create situations in which tragedy is inevitable.'

She concluded with an exhortation to her stricken audience. 'Sorrow in our hearts must be turned into constructive channels. Let us resolve to carry on the work for which Mr Dag Hammarskjoeld gave his life. Let us make the United Nations a powerful force for good and an effective and dynamic instrument for peace. To this end let us devote our energies. No man is perfect, but Dag's life and his death have added immensely to the dignity and worth of the whole human race, and it is in the hearts and conscience of humanity that he will find an enduring memorial.'

142 *Envoy Extraordinary*

For a time complete physical exhaustion had given Vijaya Lakshmi the idea that retirement into private life would be agreeable. Before her brother's telephone call asking her to attend Dag Hammarskjoeld's funeral, she had fallen ill in Greece and moved to Cairo to stay with her daughter Rita, where she had spent a month recuperating in bed.

On her return to India from Stockholm she took a small flat in Mafatlal Park, Bombay, the great industrial city facing the palm-fringed Arabian Sea, with its modern hotels, textile factories, huge concrete blocks of workers' tenements and continuous assemblies of middle-class flats. Here, where the distant blue outline of the Western Ghats dominated the eastern horizon, she dreamed of building a country home near the Himalayas where her grandchildren could visit her, and perhaps eventually sharing it with Jawaharlal when he retired.

She visualized the place as Dehra Dun, their favourite hill station near Delhi where there was ample space and a background of abundant woods, and hoped he would join her there for some final years of quiet. The previous year he had said to Arthur Cook of the *Daily Mail*: 'I want to see the job finished, but who knows how much longer I can go on, maybe one year, maybe two or three. I feel I would like a quieter time.'

Living obscurely as a private citizen which she had not been for years, Vijaya Lakshmi was able to compare the India of 1961 with the tumultuous country on the verge of Independence which she had left for Moscow in August 1947. She saw remarkable economic progress combined with ever-threatening political disunity.

'Somehow,' she said to a friend in 1963, 'politics had not marched abreast with economics.'

Though India's past failure to catch up with the Industrial Revolution had left her still dominated by nation-wide poverty, the economic changes were visible and tangible. New buildings and bridges were everywhere to be seen, and loitering cows and buffaloes, now rounded up into community farms, no longer impeded traffic on the clearly-marked modern main roads. Many of the once primitive Government guest-houses had been replaced by well-designed structures with up-to-date furniture, though sanitation still tended to lag behind other forms of modernization. The old floor-type toilets had only sporadic-ally been replaced by Western-style plumbing, and where this existed it was seldom efficient; the proudly-exhibited occasional flush system tended to immerse the user in a deluge of cold water.

A large increase of hospitals and clinics counterbalanced the pains-taking but poor sanitation. The frequent animals, especially dogs, now

## Bombay and After 143

ambling beside rather than on the highways, seemed better fed and better treated, and were now seldom disease-ridden. Though most railway carriages were still old-fashioned, slow, and dust-covered, a few fast air-conditioned trains linked the chief capital cities, while all over the country air-terminals both large and small had sprung up like outsize mushrooms. In many previous desert areas irrigation had brought well-being to some villages, though India as a whole still showed few signs of prosperity.

Social changes had followed in the wake of economic advance. The caste system had been greatly modified since Independence under the new Constitution which forbade discrimination on grounds of caste, race, religion, sex, or birth-location. The Community Development movement had been extended to the decentralization, known as *Panchayat Raj*, in favour of village-elected councils which had considerable authority. The integration of the old princely States with the country as a whole had taken away much of the former pageantry and pomp, but had brought a new equality in both theory and practice. Some scions of princely families, such as the Maharajah of Bikaner and the Maharanee of Jaipur, had identified themselves with India's Government and become Members of Parliament.

She learned that the pupils in the primary schools had more than doubled. The university students had multiplied by five, which meant that India, though gradually moving into the modern world, would preserve her noble heritage of religion, literature and scholarship. Women especially had made remarkable progress. In the middle classes many girls now trained themselves for careers who, like their Victorian British counterparts, would previously have been content to stay at home occupied by minor domestic duties, or to marry very young and bring up large families.

Yes, she felt, the gigantic tasks that faced India after the British left had been tackled with courage and dedication, yet politics did not appear to her to have kept pace with social and economic change. People were thinking and talking loosely, and it seemed to her that the threat to Indian unity had grown since the days when the struggle for Independence had united both sexes and all classes in one great campaign. She soon became conscious of disruptive elements in Indian society— Capitalism and Communism; the potentially divisive influences of caste and religion; the ugly spectre of communal tension, and the menacing fragmentation of the Congress Party. 'I have always been among those,' she said, 'who thought that for the present India's rôle was at home . . . Unless our best minds and talents are given over to meeting this situa-

144 *Envoy Extraordinary*

tion, we shall not be able to play a leading rôle on the international plane. Our strength as well as our leadership in the world can only be derived from our traditions and background.'

The contrast which Vijaya Lakshmi found between independent India and the turbulent country just emerging from revolution which she had left fourteen years earlier, emphasized for her the personal changes which had come to her relatives and friends. Her brother, though the renal ailment which was to plague him the following year had not yet been diagnosed and he still marched in the Republic Day parade, was clearly a tired man who no longer bounded up staircases and talked with affectionate gaiety to the perpetual Greek Chorus of his admirers. Her daughters had long grown up and married and were distributed over the world; even their children were reaching school age. Her niece Indira, in 1947 a young woman of thirty married five years earlier and absorbed in the care of two small sons, Rajiv and Sanjay, had been for fourteen years Jawaharlal's hostess in Delhi and was transformed by the experience.

Initially moulded by the constant adversity of her early youth, dominated by visits from the police and her father's frequent absences in prison, she was now a beautiful, mature woman of forty-four and a seasoned if always reluctant politician. In 1959 she had been an effective President of Congress when no one else was willing to assume the position, though she had resigned the office after serving for a year. At times Vijaya Lakshmi would wonder uncomfortably how far her own continuing, though temporarily relinquished, aspirations towards active politics would fit in with the intentions of this quiet but strong-willed heiress-apparent, who might not prove accommodating either as politician or relative.

Whatever the future prospects for India might be, Nehru's daughter would never be a negligible factor; in some future crisis her wishes and choices might well be determinant.

Vijaya Lakshmi had not been back in India three months when the crisis which resulted in India's seizure of Goa disturbed and even horrified her British friends.

Goa, a beautiful palm-dotted territory of 1,300 square miles situated on the coast of Western India, had first been occupied by the Portuguese in 1510. Its uncomfortable status now emphasized the problems created for modern India by the last set of enclaves on Indian soil which had been tolerated by the British authorities. The inevitable inclusion of Goa in India had been postponed by a 1952 declaration by

## Bombay and After 145

Portugal's Minister of Overseas Territories that 'Goa was part and parcel of Metropolitan Portugal', though the enclave was scathingly described in India as 'decadant colonialism facing resurgent Asia'.

For several years the Goan national movement inside the picturesque little territory had been gaining strength. The moral problems involved became the subject of Parliamentary debate; in the Lower House on July 26, 1955, the unrepentant Gandhian, Acharya Kripalani, had asked directly whether the Government of India was pledged to non-violence. Jawaharlal replied bluntly that the answer was No.

'As far as I can conceive, under the existing circumstances, no Government can be pledged to non-violence ... One may have an ideal. One may adhere to a policy leading in a certain direction and yet, because of existing circumstances, one cannot give effect to that ideal.'[1]

On August 15, 1955, a hundred volunteers had entered Goa in a mass *satyagraha* campaign, which had resulted in several being shot or beaten by Portuguese police. Three days later India severed consular relations with Goa, but went on trying to solve the problem peacefully. On August 16, 1961, two Portuguese enclaves within Goa were formally declared part of the Indian Union at their own request, but Portuguese rule over the territory as a whole continued. On October 26th, Jawaharlal, losing the patience which was never his paramount quality, said in Bombay: 'We have been criticized for the delay in freeing Goa because of our policy of peace ... We have been forced into thinking afresh by the Portuguese ... I have no doubt that Goa will soon be free.'

In December 1961, when Indian military action against Goa seemed imminent, a contingent of Press correspondents settled down on the borders of the territory, but were prevented by a Government officer from moving in with the Army. This prohibition, later alleged to be due to misjudgment by the Defence Minister, Krishna Menon, meant the exclusion of sympathetic Indian reporters, while a number of hostile foreign journalists found their way in. Hence one-sided reports were given to the world emphasizing the degree to which Jawaharlal had compromised with violence in the interests of India.[2] On December 18th he ordered Indian troops to march into Goa, and by sheer military might drove out the Portuguese.[3]

Vijaya Lakshmi's ever-present anxiety for her brother was not dis-

[1] Lok Sabha, July 26, 1955. *India's Foreign Policy*, p. 115. (Publications Division, Ministry of Information and Broadcasting, Government of India.)

[2] T. J. G. George, *Krishna Menon*, pp. 231-2.

[3] Goa eventually became a part of India on December 19, 1962, when Major-General K. P. Gandreth was appointed its Military Governor.

K

146                    *Envoy Extraordinary*

pelled by the international repercussions. A *Times* editorial commented severely, if correctly, on the 'setback' to India's policy of peaceful solutions, and an *Evening Standard* article[1] by the young poet, Dom Moraes, son of Gandhi's biographer Frank Moraes, struck a sorrowful note: 'I am an Indian, and on this day I cannot but feel ashamed.'

The previous day Krishna Menon, explosively angry at the United Nations with critics who talked of 'aggression' by India, demanded an apology from reporters, and a week later Sunder Kabadi, of London's Indian Press, recalled to the readers of the *Guardian* Gandhi's dictum when Pakistan raided Kashmir: 'I don't like violence but slavery is worse.' An article in the same newspaper by Lord Altrincham (John Grigg) probably summed up correctly Britain's long-range judgment on Nehru's action in Goa: 'A saint may inspire his people, but only a statesman can actually govern a country.'[2]

So far the wish expressed by the author of this book in a letter to Vijaya Lakshmi when she left for India[3]—'Hoping so much that your own country will give you more opportunities for peace and quiet than ours did'—had hardly materialized. As the dust from the Goan turmoil gradually settled, Vijaya Lakshmi's thoughts turned to India's third General Election, due to be contested in February 1962 and certain to be influenced by the recent crisis. One of its direct consequences was a ferocious election fight in Bombay between Acharya Kripalani and Krishna Menon, which resulted in Menon's overwhelming victory on March 3, 1962, by a majority of 145,367 votes. Whatever the Western world might think of the Goan *fait accompli*, the reactions of Western India were left in no doubt.

Jawaharlal Nehru regarded the recently-formed Swatantra Party, dominated by the aged Rajagopalachari, the former Governor-General, as the most serious challenge to the Socialist edifice which was the new India of his own creation. Yet it seemed certain that Congress, though impaired by faction fights and petty squabbles, would again be returned to power by the 210 million voters who constituted the largest free election of all time. Forty per cent of these voters were now literate, as against only twelve per cent when Independence came. Though divided by their different faiths, languages and tribes, they had helped Jawaharlal to lay the foundations of a modern industrial State.

On February 3rd, in the midst of the Election, Vijaya Lakshmi received the Republic Day award known as the Padma Vibhushan,

[1] December 21, 1961.
[2] *Guardian*, December 21, 1961.
[3] October 13, 1961.

## Bombay and After 147

given to distinguished Indians who had won recognition in various fields. Another recipient was the daughter of the late Mrs Sarojini Naidu, Miss Padmaja Naidu, who was now Governor of West Bengal. Three months later, following the retirement as President of Dr Rajendra Prasad, came the election of a new President, Dr Sarvepalli Radhakrishnan (Sir Sarvepalli in Britain), the distinguished philosopher who had been for many years a Fellow of All Souls' College, Oxford. He took up his office just in time to support the Prime Minister, whose obscure complaint began to declare itself in August 1962, and eventually compelled him to seek treatment in England.

Cruelly coinciding with this period of ill-health came the Chinese invasion, which for those familiar with the mountain border territories had its origins as far back as 1954–55, when the Chinese first began to push against India's Northern frontiers. The Indian Government, its Members imbued with the Gandhian philosophy of non-violence, found the reality of this threat difficult to believe owing to the apparently sincere friendship which had so long existed between India and China.

In April 1954, an agreement between the two countries regarding Tibet had been signed in Peking between Mr N. Raghavan, the Indian Ambassador accredited to the People's Republic, and Mr Chang Han-fu, the Chinese Vice-Minister of Foreign Affairs. This agreement laid down Five Principles of peaceful co-existence which later came to be known as 'Panchsheel'.[1] Thereafter, for a time, the traditional friendship between India and China so long symbolized by the 'Cheena Bhawan' in Tagore's University at Santiniketan, seemed to flourish as before.

During 1955 Krishna Menon, who had become friendly with Chou En-lai at both Geneva and Bandung, visited China and succeeded in arranging the release of four American airmen recently shot down near the Chinese coast and imprisoned as spies. That same year India welcomed Chou En-lai to Delhi and invited him again in 1960, though by that time Jawaharlal referred at a banquet held in the visitor's honour to the 'serious disagreements' which 'have unfortunately arisen between us'.

The previous year, India and China had clashed over the question of sovereignty in Tibet, and China had been responsible for incursions

---

[1] The Five Principles were: (a) Mutual respect for each other's territorial integrity and sovereignty; (b) Mutual non-aggression; (c) Mutual non-interference in each other's internal affairs; (d) Equality and mutual benefit; (e) Peaceful co-existence. Nehru himself had formulated these principles, which formed the preamble to the agreement.

148                    *Envoy Extraordinary*

across India's frontier in the mountainous Ladahk area where even the valleys reached an altitude of 13,000 feet. At the 1960 banquet in New Delhi, Jawaharlal referred to the long-standing friendship between Asia's two dominant nations: 'Thousands of years of two great and ancient civilizations stand witness to our meeting, and the hopes of hundreds of millions for a happier future are tied up in our endeavours.'[1]

Violations of the long lofty frontier nevertheless continued, and relations steadily worsened until in September 1962, when Vijaya Lakshmi was mourning Dag Hammarskjoeld in Sweden, a series of major incursions by the Chinese began. On October 20th a massive attack started against territory claimed as Indian in the North-east Frontier Agency and Ladahk, which Indian troops unaccustomed both to war, and to the high altitudes and sub-zero temperature of mountain battlefields, could do no more than resist with tragic, ineffective valour. When the invaders captured the key town of Tawang in the North-east Frontier Agency on October 25th, the Prime Minister declared a state of emergency. Numbed and shaken, the Indian people made both Jawaharlal and Krishna Menon, the Defence Minister, the targets of their wrath, and early in November Menon resigned from the Cabinet.

'It is my hope,' Vijaya Lakshmi had written in a Foreword to the 1960 issue of India's magazine *Foreign Affairs,* 'that India may be able to face whatever comes to her with strength and dignity.'

Now, all over the country, alarmed and helpless citizens were praying the same prayer. Suddenly, on November 21st, with British families leaving the threatened Assam tea-plantations for England, the Chinese in their overwhelming numbers strangely resorted to unilateral cease-fire, and withdrew from the advance areas that they had occupied. India was left bewildered and uncertain, mobilizing all her available human and material resources to resist a fate which was none the less terrifying because it had become so difficult to define.[2]

Before the alarm created by the Chinese invasion had reached its peak, Vijaya Lakshmi left India for a visit to the West. On October 23rd she opened an International Hall of Residence which was the result of a

---

[1] *India's Foreign Policy*, p. 384.

[2] Three months after the invasion the author of this book and her husband, visiting Formosa (a valuable back-door source of information on China) by invitation of old friends of the Second World War during a short tour of Asia, put a direct question to responsible Free Chinese officials in Teipeh: 'Why did China attack India and then withdraw in the midst of a successful campaign?' The threefold answer was illuminating: (1) To preserve the Sinkiang-Tibet road going through Ladahk; (2) To increase Chinese prestige in South-east Asia; (3) To demonstrate that Mr Nehru was not so important as he had appeared, though the Chinese Government did not wish actually to displace him.

## Bombay and After 149

remarkable co-operative effort between the British Government, London University, and twenty-one overseas Governments (all from the Commonwealth except Austria). Of these Governments India, in sending £30,000, had made the largest contribution. This impressive modern hostel in Brunswick Square, with rooms for 271 men students, had grown from a suggestion by the late Sir Samuel Ranganadhan, India's High Commissioner in London from 1943 to 1947.

In her speech opening the hostel Vijaya Lakshmi did not refer to the fighting on India's borders, but emphasized that in this 'age of investment any investment in human beings is the highest and safest investment any nation can have.' She did, however, mentioned the frontier war in an address to the YMCA Indian students on October 25th, and commented that the point at issue was not just a matter of barren border territory.

'It is, in effect, a crystallization of the battle for Asia,' she said. 'In my opinion, we have to decide at this time whether we are prepared to stand up for what we believe, or whether we are not.' She added that she had never seen the ordinary people of India so deeply concerned about anything as the Chinese invasion.

'They cannot see why we talk of a peaceful solution at a moment when our men are dying. If even this much had happened in any other country, there would have been war before now. But patience and tolerance are not enough; we must face the situation. Since the last war we have gradually come to accept as normal the Cold War and the series of small wars. We must not allow apathy to develop. We are walking on a tight-rope, and a war could start without anybody wanting a war.'

'Try,' she concluded, 'to work out our common beliefs, so that at least we may face what lies in store as a united people.'

From London she spent eleven days in Germany, where she laid the foundation stone of a new India House in Düsseldorf, the first of its kind in Continental Europe, and went on to Bonn for talks with Chancellor Adenauer, President Heinrich Luebe, and the Economic Minister, Dr Ludwig Erhard. Before leaving the West for her important new position as Governor of Maharashtra—an appointment which followed the death of the former Governor, Dr P. Sabbaroyan—she gave a final talk in London to the Overseas League in which she described China's attack—the 'stab in the back' by a friend with whom her country had felt a spiritual affinity—as 'a wound on India's soul'.

Her Government, she said, had worked so hard to raise the living

150    *Envoy Extraordinary*

standards of India's people by democratic means, rather than by the short cuts characteristic of totalitarian States. She didn't like all the changes she had found in India, though she had begun to feel that she 'belonged' again. She had been drawn back to England by 'the values by which British people try to live'—those qualities of the spirit which included the moral courage so much needed by India today. No country, she concluded, had experienced a more chequered history than her own—'but India has not endured for thousands of years to go down now'.

Her new appointment was not one which she faced with enthusiasm; politics—and fighting politics—were the breath of her life. She had become too closely acclimatized to the delicately-balanced international battles which major diplomacy involved to be greatly attracted by a figurehead position, however imposing. Even to be the Governor of India's largest State, with responsibility for an area of 190,919 square miles and a population of nearly 50 million inhabitants, did not offer the positive opportunities of which she had learned so well how to take advantage.[1]

But she had realized, since returning to India, that life as a private citizen would never bring fulfilment; she had felt 'out of things' in the small flat in Mafatlal Park. So she had accepted the Governorship of Maharashtra in the hope that more active work would ultimately present itself, and moved into the beautiful Raj Bhawan, once the home of Bombay's British Governors who had never economized on their own surroundings.

The huge former province of Bombay had been divided into the separate States of Maharashtra and Gujerat in response to popular demand. Neither State wanted to relinquish Bombay city, but eventually it remained the capital of Maharashtra while Gujerat decided to build a new capital. Taking charge on November 28, 1962, Vijaya Lakshmi established herself on the southern point of Malabar Hill, between Back Bay and the Arabian Sea. Across the Bay she could see the majestic sweep of the Marine Drive, with its night-time glitter of lights popularly known as 'the Queen's necklace'.

Below the perfectly-situated residence surged and swung the Arabian Sea, always rough at the shore's edge, making a soothing lullaby sound all day and night. White-painted balustrades with black-flecked yellow stone floors ran all round the main house, a series of one-storey struc-

---

[1] She resigned from the Governorship in October 1964 to fight the by-election for Mr Nehru's seat at Phulpur, near Allahabad.

## Bombay and After

151

tures following the shape of the cliffs. The colourful buildings had red-tiled roofs and verandah blinds of blue-green coconut matting. Smoothly-mown lawns sloped steeply down towards the sea above the sheer rough rocks. At intervals flower-beds stocked with tall coral-pink cannas, and small firs with leaves like thin shoelaces, broke the green evenness of the grass. White sea-birds flew perpetually over the water, and squawking crows periodically occupied the garden. A few richly-hued butterflies flitted above the decorative cannas. If Vijaya Lakshmi had been looking for an earthly paradise unimpaired by the restless turmoil of political aspirations and alarms, she could have found it in this fairy-tale mansion.

In Bombay she was over a thousand miles from Calcutta and 1,200 from the menaced plantations of Assam, yet the threat of war hung like an imminent nightmare over the crowded city where war posters urged the working population: 'Do not strike work, strike for defence'. Yet, conscious though she always was of her brother's problems and the half-explicit, half-suspended criticism of the anxious millions over whom he ruled, it was now neither war nor defence nor the stressful relations with China which had to be her main concern.

As she was to tell the joint session of the Maharashtra Legislature in her first address to them on February 12, 1963—when she wore the white sari customary on official occasions—the State Government, as part of its defence effort, had drawn up a detailed, integrated plan for stepping up industrial and agricultural production. But here, apart from continually encouraging collections for the Defence Fund, her connection with the external relations of her State came to an end.

The office of Governor, normally lasting for a term of five years from the date of appointment, chiefly involved a variety of local obligations such as the making of laws in consultation with a Council of Ministers, the exercise of 'discretion' in the solution of State problems, the granting of pardons or remission of punishments, the administration of oaths of office and of secrecy to new Ministers entering upon their duties, the appointment of the State Advocate-General, and the institution of rules 'for the more convenient transaction of the business of the government of the State and the allocations of such business among Ministers'.[1]

The Governor had also the task of summoning and addressing the Legislative Assembly, and could further vary her constitutional duties by nominating as members of the Legislative Council 'persons having special knowledge or practical experience in such matters as literature,

[1] From *The Constitution of India*, as modified up to March 1, 1963.

152 *Envoy Extraordinary*

science, art, the co-operative movement, and social service'. From the more decorative social standpoint her position involved attendance at outstanding local functions, such as banquets, official luncheons and teas, and even sporting events in any part of the State. She had also to entertain distinguished visitors, and arrange for them to be met and seen off at Bombay Airport or the main railway terminal.

After nine months of this semi-legal, semi-social régime, carried out beneath the threat of invasion which did not develop further though there was no escaping from its significance as propaganda, she was glad to be given the opportunity of a return to diplomacy. On August 17, 1963, the eve of her birthday, her appointment was announced as leader of India's delegation to the Eighteenth General Assembly of the United Nations after ten uninterrupted years in which Krishna Menon had been the chief Indian spokesman.

'Mr Menon's replacement became inevitable after his elimination from the Indian Government last fall when the Chinese Communists invaded the country,' reported the *New York Times* on August 19th, 'but Mrs Pandit's nomination is seen as an indication of Prime Minister Nehru's own recent movement towards the West... Unlike Mr Menon, who succeeded in antagonizing the West almost every time he spoke, Mrs Pandit managed to follow India's non-alignment policy and remain friends with both sides in the cold war.'

She left India in the first week of September to revisit Ghana after five years, on the way to New York. It was perhaps of Ghana, as much as of any other have-not country, including her own, that she had declared in the United States a few years earlier that a world 'half-oxcart and half-Cadillac' was doomed. One woman journalist, observing her at the United Nations during that autumn's session, described her as 'rather tired perhaps of the often pointless manoeuvres of the latter-day Afro-Asians; disappointed too that so few members of the UN have a clear understanding of India's attitude to her dispute with Pakistan, and of the reasons which prompt India's fears of Communist China.'

At a Press Conference in New York on September 13th both these questions were raised, and Vijaya Lakshmi commented with unwonted asperity, probably based on official instructions, that year after year India had been making one concession after another to Pakistan in the hope of reaching amicable relations but she had arrived at a point where she was not prepared to make any more. She appeared to be truer to her normal character when she remarked that India still believed that China should have a seat in the United Nations and that this question had nothing to do with India's current relations with China.

## Bombay and After 153

Nine days later, another interview in the National Broadcasting Corporation's programme 'Meet the Press' brought her back to the perennial question of South Africa which she had first raised at the United Nations in October 1946. India, she now said, would vote for the expulsion of South Africa from the world body if the question came up there. There was, she insisted, no contradiction between India's attitude on this point and the need for seating China, which involved a strict adherence to the letter and spirit of the UN Charter.

There was no doubt, she added, that the expulsion of South Africa in itself would lead to nothing and might be a useless step, but India would none the less vote for expulsion, because 'the people of Asia and Africa regard South Africa's *apartheid* policies as worse than any territorial aggression'. Black and brown nations, she concluded, unequivocally, were in a majority at the United Nations today, and were not prepared to accept inferiority because of their black or brown skin. This indignity was something which these people 'would not tolerate, forgive, or forget'.

On September 30, 1963, Vijaya Lakshmi exercised her 'right of reply' at the United Nations to 'serious allegations' made against India by Pakistan.

'The Foreign Minister of Pakistan has said that the central issue in Kashmir is that of self-determination and that both parties accepted this. I would like to deny categorically here and now this assertion of the Foreign Minister of Pakistan. And I would like to add, with all the authority of the Government of India, that the issue in Kashmir is one of aggression, of Pakistani aggression, committed in 1947 and 1948 and which continues to this day.'

In a long speech she reviewed, with the passion of a Kashmiri Brahmin added to 'the authority of the Government of India', the tangled and unhappy history of India and Pakistan over the previous fifteen years. Western delegates listened, as always, to this baffling story with the discomfort of representatives whose own record of near-neighbour relationships did not entitle them to sit in judgment.

Six days later she added to her still growing total of honorary Degrees a Doctorate of Humane Letters awarded by Brandeis University, Massachusetts. The academic citation said of her that 'she moves gracefully and graciously through complexities of government and international affairs . . . a first lady of the world in a tradition that this university has come to treasure.'

Further references to the aggressive policies of both China and

# 154 — *Envoy Extraordinary*

Pakistan occurred before the General Assembly on October 11th in another speech which, without being conciliatory, put the relations between Pakistan, China and India constructively into perspective. Insisting that 'there can be no greater calamity for us than conflict with Pakistan,' she continued: 'All that we want to ensure is that, brothers that we are, we live in peace with one another, that the upheaval and unsettlement that we witnessed at our birth should never again recur.' Going on to discuss China, she added:

'China and India are the two largest countries of Asia and share between them a population of more than one billion—which is more than one-third of the total world population. If there is conflict between them there can be no peace in Asia. On both India and China, therefore, devolves a great responsibility.'

More wholly in accordance with her own 'graceful and gracious' tradition was the speech pleading for a total Test-Ban Treaty with which she opened the debate on October 25th in the Political Committee. Discussing the India-sponsored item for banning nuclear tests, she described the Moscow Partial Test-Ban Treaty as a first step and recognized that underground testing still remained to be banned. She then begged the General Assembly to exercise all the moral pressure at its command to persuade dissident countries to sign the Treaty.

'A very large portion of the world breathes more easily because this Treaty—limited though it be—has been signed.' India, she said, regretted that France had felt unable to sign it, while the People's Republic of China had launched a bitterly hostile campaign which called the Treaty 'a big fraud to fool the peoples of the world.'

'This kind of perverse thinking,' she remarked, 'can only be understood when seen against the peculiar philosophy which views the destruction of hundreds of millions of human beings in a nuclear holocaust with equanimity . . . Our purpose,' she concluded, 'is not to drive the nuclear arms race underground, but to end it.'

Two weeks later she followed this speech by a statement in the First Committee on the importance of general and complete disarmament, in which she compared the Soviet and American plans for this purpose in a speech which showed detailed technical knowledge of both. She welcomed the newly established direct communication link between Moscow and Washington, paid tribute to the work of the Eighteen Nation Committee in Geneva, and emphasized how far the expectations of people who hoped for a disarmed world were centred in the United Nations.

*Bombay and After* 155

In November she returned to the same theme at a luncheon in the Carnegie International Endowment for Peace Centre, and argued that the Non-Governmental Organizations associated with the UN should increasingly devote their energies to disarmament, for 'quiet constructive work is more important in public affairs than brilliance . . . And the good can prevent nuclear disaster from happening, provided we are not afraid.'

She ended her talk with a remarkable Asian story.

'A good king rode out from his city one fine morning in the autumn to hunt. On the road he met Death riding towards his city. He wished to turn back and warn his people, but Death said it would make no difference whatever, that he had a mission to fulfil, and a hundred persons must die whether or not the king was there. But he promised that no more than one hundred would be taken. The king rode on in sorrow. He had no heart for the hunt. Empty-handed he returned at sunset to a silent city. It was like a tomb. It was a city of the dead.

'At the gate stood Death. "What have you done?" asked the king. "I kept my promise, believe me. I took less than a hundred of your people." "Then how is it that all my people are dead?" demanded the king. "The rest died by my brother's hand," said Death. "My brother's name is Fear." '

On October 21st Vijaya Lakshmi was invited to pay a tribute to Eleanor Roosevelt at the Lincoln Centre, New York City, on the first anniversary of her death. As she spoke of her own affection for Mrs Roosevelt, many memories came back—of America's support during India's freedom struggle; of the endeavour they had shared in later years to increase justice and opportunity through the United Nations; of the gavel presented to her by Mrs Roosevelt when she herself was President. Eleanor Roosevelt, she concluded, had been much blessed.

'To have been able to serve the causes she believed in, to have inspired men and women in all parts of the world, to have strengthened so many through her friendship, to have seen some of her labours completed—these are things which rarely happen in one life. When they do come together, the person does not die.'

A month after this tribute came a day of triumph, followed swiftly by major disaster. On November 21st the General Assembly, by acclamation, approved a Resolution which designated 1965 as International Co-operation Year, in which twelve months would be set aside to examine ways and means by which international co-operation might

# 156 Envoy Extraordinary

be increased. The acceptance of this Resolution without dissension, though all the delegates had different views of what it implied, brought great joy to Vijaya Lakshmi since the idea had originally been proposed by her brother in November 1961. But satisfaction and rejoicing turned swiftly to tragedy the next afternoon, when the United Nations was numbed and shattered by the news of President Kennedy's assassination.

It proved impossible to send anyone from India in time for his funeral on November 25th, and Vijaya Lakshmi was appointed to attend it with the Indian Ambassador to Washington on behalf of President Radhakrishnan. With the rulers of the world gathered together in mourning, she stood close to the coffin in Arlington cemetery on that bitter November morning. Having so recently paid tribute to a great woman whose life had been fulfilled, she now joined her colleagues at the Memorial meeting of the General Assembly on November 26th to speak sorrowfully of the brilliant and still young life cut off in the midst of full achievement. In terms of its crucial effect on world history, she saw his assassination as parallel to the martyrdom of Mahatma Gandhi.

'Three shots fired in Dallas, Texas, on November 22, 1963, took one's mind back to three other shots fired on a January afternoon in India fifteen years ago, when Mahatma Gandhi became a victim of the assassin's bullet. Though the time and place were different, the deed in both cases represented the ascendancy, for the moment, of the powers of hatred and violence which both Mahatma Gandhi and John Fitzgerald Kennedy fought against all their lives.

'The hands that struck these men had hoped, not only to end their lives, but to strike a blow at the ideals they stood for. But fifteen years after the death of Gandhi, his life and message continue to guide and strengthen people not only in India but everywhere in the world.

'President Kennedy had become a symbol of the values he so unswervingly upheld, and there is not the slightest doubt that his message will be a source of unending inspiration to future generations in every part of the globe. He was prophetic when he said in his Inaugural address that "The torch has been passed on to a new generation of Americans". This torch is the legacy he has left to his country and to the world . . . Mankind will cherish his luminous and fragrant memory . . . We pray that in spite of the insanity by which we seem to be momentarily surrounded, the spirit of love will triumph over hate and that John Fitzgerald Kennedy's death will not have been in vain.'

Her final speech in the Security Council as Chairman of the Indian

## Bombay and After 157

Delegation on November 29th referred once more to that hardy annual of her political lifetime, the South African policy of *apartheid* on which she had addressed the first session of the First General Assembly precisely seventeen years earlier. Though the 'mild resolution' which then resulted had made 'a chink in South Africa's armour', the South African Government still moved from one hideous act to another.

'Gradually a climate is being created in which the growing hate and frustration will lead, inevitably, to violence and even war . . . Nothing can take the place of the feeling of equality between man and man which must exist if the world is to survive. Must another war be fought before South Africa mends its ways?'

With passionate courage she appealed to the world's major trading countries to end the perpetual crisis by exercising their power, and quoted Chief Albert Luthuli's book, *Let My People Go,* to show that the Africans themselves were prepared for such personal sacrifices as the economic boycott of South Africa would involve.

'It is the developed nations of the West who have to make up their minds and put an end to all trade with South Africa. The time for half-measures and stop-gap arrangements is over . . . It is at once a matter of regret and surprise to us that some nations sitting around this table, while condemning the racial policies of South Africa continue to have massive trade with that country . . . All trade has to stop, and the lead for this has to come from the United Kingdom and the United States.'

As soon as the most eventful, tragic and strenuous Assembly that even she had ever attended came to an end she hastened back to India, where the news of her brother's rapidly failing health and its political repercussions had caused her growing concern. His seventy-fourth birthday had been celebrated on November 14th, but his hold on the Premiership seemed as firm as ever, and no one took seriously any of his potential rivals.

Not until a frank and startling article by Tom Stacey appeared in the London *Sunday Times* for January 5, 1964, did the half-indifferent international world begin to realize how soon Jawaharlal's successor would probably have to be chosen. The photograph that accompanied the article showed a familiar face suddenly grown old, with an indeterminate profile and a drooping lip—the visible and painful consequence of the Chinese invasion.

Two days later came the news that he was 'too tired and weak' to continue attending the Party sessions at the Conference in Orissa to

# 158 Envoy Extraordinary

which he had travelled. In another two days came the guarded admission of 'a mild stroke', and he was advised to remain at the Governor's House in Bhubaneswar instead of returning to Delhi.

By January 13th he was able to go home, but not to work; the Home Minister Mr G. L. Nanda and the Finance Minister Mr T. T. Krishnamachari shared the duties of leadership. Talk of the next Prime Minister involved references to Indira Gandhi, but both she and her father resisted the proposal though a seat in the Cabinet was suggested for her as a period of trial during the Prime Minister's lifetime. It seemed rather that Mr Lal Bahadur Shastri was in process of being 'evolved'.

While Jawaharlal suffered two serious losses of old colleagues and advisers—the Sardar K. H. Panikkar, India's historian, had died in Mysore on December 10, 1963, and Rajkumari Amrit Kaur (described by the London *Times* as 'one of the three great women thrown up by the nationalist movement[1]) followed him in February 1964—he himself seemed gradually to recover. On March 30th he rejected the suggestion that he might appoint a Deputy Prime Minister, and in April he was able to see Sheik Abdullah, the former State Prime Minister of Kashmir who had been released from prison only a fortnight before he became Jawaharlal's guest.

The discussion over the future of Jammu and Kashmir was still continuing early in May, when his host decided that he had now recovered sufficiently from his illness to take a brief holiday at Dehra Dun.

[1] The others were Sarojini Naidu and Vijaya Lakshmi herself.

CHAPTER 12

# Nightfall on the Jumna

'This is the true joy in life, the being used for a purpose recognized by yourself as a mighty one; the being thoroughly worn out before you are thrown on the scrap heap.'

Bernard Shaw, *Man and Superman.*

THERE seemed to be no reason why Jawaharlal should not pay this short visit to the Himalayan foothills which he had always loved, even though the journey involved two flights by helicopter over the mountainous country.

It was true that he had never fully recovered from the virus infection which had damaged his kidneys in March 1962, and the minor stroke that he suffered in January had caused a momentary occlusion[1] which for a time affected his left arm and leg. But from the beginning of March he had been able to attend Parliament regularly; had recently travelled to the borders of Nepal to meet the king; and early in May had visited Bombay for a session of the All-India Congress Committee.

Here he told his hearers some blunt home truths about Hindu violence to Muslims in secular India, and spoke of a Belgian priest killed in Bihar because he had tried to protect Muslims against Hindu attackers. The courage that this criticism demanded was revealed by the meagre applause which greeted his speech in contrast to the ovation before he began, but his weakness and weariness commanded the reverence of the committee members in spite of the promptings of fanaticism. A party colleague tried to help him when he rose to speak, but Jawaharlal brushed him aside, ignored a special chair and shortened microphone prepared for him on the platform, and went resolutely to the full-length standing microphone used by the other speakers.

When he returned from Dehra Dun on May 22nd, he told the Press that he had 'given some thought' to a suggestion that he should retire as Premier and play the elder statesman's rôle of adviser. He had already

[1] A blood stoppage in the brain.

# 160 — Envoy Extraordinary

announced his intention of going to the Commonwealth Prime Ministers' Conference in London in July, for he had attended every such Conference since 1947. To the journalist who had questioned him about his retirement he commented bluntly: 'My life time is not ending so very soon.'

It was his final challenge to impending fate. On Tuesday evening, May 26th, he went to bed in apparently normal health. As usual he rose at dawn, but almost immediately complained of pain in his back. Shortly afterwards, smitten by a second stroke and a simultaneous heart attack he lapsed into unconsciousness, and though he was placed under oxygen he did not respond. At 11.45 a.m.[1] the Home Minister, Mr Nanda, reported his serious illness to Parliament. Two and a quarter hours later he died, with Indira at his bedside. In Parliament the Minister for Steel, Mr C. Subramaniam, told the weeping Members: 'The Prime Minister is no more. Life is out. The light is out.'[2]

Within minutes the news of his death was known throughout Delhi and was soon carried all over India, but word of his illness had not reached Vijaya Lakshmi in Bombay in time for her to be with him at the last. Though she summoned a special aircraft, she reached the Prime Minister's house only as the first mourners were already filing through it. Indira, in the white robes of Hindu mourning, her head covered by a sari, sat on the floor beside her father's bed.

Two months afterwards, in a letter dated July 9, 1964, Vijaya Lakshmi wrote to the author of her own response to those fateful days.

'The whole of the last month has passed like a nightmare. My brother had been ill from the time he had his kidney trouble two years ago but he seemed to have things in control. The stroke last January, mild though it was, left no doubt that he could not carry the heavy burden of responsibility he had shouldered in the past. He was, however, reluctant to give up and I think I can understand.

'He co-operated with the doctors and was very good, but he kept on attacking tasks which were demanding and beyond his strength. I think he had made up his mind to go this way and even though my heart grieves and there seems to be emptiness everywhere, I thank God that he died as he had wished to do, peacefully and working to the end.

'I have been saddened by the way in which much of the British Press has belittled his work but it was good to read the many expressions of

---

[1] 7.15 a.m. London time.
[2] Some doctors held that the journey to Dehra Dun and the rough rides at high altitudes had been too much for his strength.

## Nightfall on the Jumna 161

real understanding and appreciation that were made so spontaneously.'[1] The shock of Jawaharlal's death descended upon the East and its peoples like a great cataclysm beyond comprehension or description; it seemed to be symbolized by the brief earthquake which shook Delhi an hour before the final procession began. The impact of it showed that no king or president had ever made a greater impression upon the international world than this sensitive Indian who was once the recurrent prisoner of Imperial Britain.

'It is like the fall of the Himalayas for us,' graphically commented Mr Rabindranath Gupta, the Public Relations Officer at London's India House. Shops closed all over Asia, and national flags flew at half-mast.

Throughout the day and most of the night of May 27th, Jawaharlal's body lay between huge blocks of ice in the sultry spring heat, which rose by day to 110°. It rested in the porch of his house on a trestle, covered with lilies, roses and marigolds, and was tilted so that the crowds could see his face. A board covered with purple bougainvillea protected it from the sun, and a red mark of sandalwood paste empha-

---

[1] This letter came in reply to one that I wrote her the day after Jawaharlal's death:

'I hesitate to follow our cable by a letter which will add its burden to the hundreds that you will receive. But I realize from my researches how great your private griefs have been, and this last, a sorrow's crown of sorrow which you share with all India but which is yet peculiarly your own, will I know be heavier and more bitter than the others . . .

'As surely as any soldier on the frontier, your brother is a casualty of the Chinese invasion; without it, he would undoubtedly have carried on his work for many years. Like Gandhi he is a victim of the violence against which they both struggled so tirelessly. "Very substantially", to use Mr Nehru's famous words, they both succeeded. India will surely follow their lead, until violence is conquered.'

I could not however wholly agree with her criticism of British newspapers, and wrote to say so on July 28th.

'I am very sorry you felt that our Press did your brother's achievements less than justice, for I did not get that impression at the time. *The Times*, for instance, had an Obituary article covering three-quarters of a page, and the *Observer* had a long appreciative essay called "The Man Behind the Saint", as well as much else. The *Sunday Times* printed long articles too, and ten days after his death published some remarkable pictures of the funeral ceremony in its Colour Supplement.

'I conclude you must have been unlucky in seeing mainly articles or quotations from Beaverbrook and Rothermere papers. . . . Yet the *Evening Standard* (a Beaverbrook paper) published the remarkable Vicky cartoon that I sent you, and it sent to Delhi for the funeral one of its best journalists, Anne Sharpley, who wrote a most moving account.

'Vijaya Lakshmi might—and doubtless did—have directed her criticisms to Chou En-lai, who blandly sent a message of regret to India—'Grieved to learn of the unfortunate death of His Excellency Mr Jawaharlal Nehru. I wish to express to you my deep condolences and sympathy.'

L

162          *Envoy Extraordinary*

sized his pallor. Two white lotuses with their stalks crossed were placed above his head.

'Our last memory of him was what he would have wished it to be—a face serene and beautiful from which the years had fallen away,' Vijaya Lakshmi wrote later to her old friend Irene Harrison. The New York *Herald-Tribune* had referred to him as 'The Great Enigma of Asia', and though he had always been her beloved brother, she had often found him an enigma too. Now, looking at his pale face so calm in death, she knew that she would never solve it; the unanswered questions which had bedevilled their relationship ever since Independence would go with her to her own life's end.

As the hours of May 27th passed, Ministers, diplomats, Members of Parliament and leading Delhi citizens filed past the white-robed body, which by Hindu custom lay facing west. Each mourner as he passed bowed his head gravely to the silent figure on the bier. Flying through the warm night came friends and representatives from England—Lord Mountbatten, the last Viceroy, with his daughter Pamela whom Jawaharlal had loved as a school-girl; the Prime Minister, Sir Alec Douglas-Home; George Brown, the deputy leader of the Opposition; Sir Paul Gore-Booth, the British High Commissioner in Delhi; Dr Jivraj Mehta, India's High Commissioner in London. But the day belonged—and was increasingly to belong when dawn came and the long scorching hours gradually lengthened towards dusk—to the common people of India.

'Through the darkness,' reported *The Times* Correspondent, 'long lines of mourners wait, many weeping, for their short chance to see again the figure that ever since India, in his words, kept its tryst with destiny and became free, has epitomized everything that was best and most hopeful in his country. Early tomorrow, near the place by the holy Jumna river, where his friend and mentor, Mahatma Gandhi, was cremated, the body of Panditji will be placed on the pyre.'

By the morning the crowds, as several journalists described them, could be measured only in square miles; they exceeded by hundreds of thousands the similar crowds which had assembled to mourn Gandhi. 'I cannot estimate a million, but millions are always recognizable,' Tom Stacey of the *Sunday Times* wrote of 'the oceanic multitude'.

'I have never,' he added, 'seen so vast a mass of human kind gazing with one mind upon anything so tiny.'

As the funeral procession moved with inevitable deliberation over the six miles which divided the Raj Path (Kingsway) of once imperial

## Nightfall on the Jumna                                      163

Delhi from the cremation ground near the half-dry Jumna river, they climbed everything they could see—the sceptred statue of King George V near the Parliament House; the dusty eucalyptus trees encircling the old Red Fort; even the great round *stupa* overlooking the Jumna meadows, with its sloping summit and no obvious method of ascent. When the procession reached this open ground, where the city's pavements gave way to almost colourless sand and arid grey-green grass, the crowd fanned out into a great human horseshoe which covered the low ridge of the meadows. There, strangely silent, only a few protected by open black umbrellas, they waited beneath the brutal impact of the afternoon sun for the ceremony which Anne Sharpley of London's *Evening Standard* called 'today's terrible immolation'.

It had to be postponed for four hours to allow the international mourners time to arrive, and like all Hindu cremations was designed to defeat the predatory vultures restlessly circling in the great pale vault of the tropical sky. Tears, sweat, and the melting *bindi* marks on the brows of the women glistened fantastically on the gentle brown faces of the ever-growing white-clad crowd, still throwing wreaths and petals towards the bier on its incongruous gun-carriage drawn by ninety Servicemen in uniform until the hot, heavy scent of jasmine dominated the windless air.

Also clad in white, Vijaya Lakshmi, her sister Krishna, and Mrs Bandaranike, the Prime Minister of Ceylon, made a small lonely group round Indira, isolated by the crowd's reverence for their private grief. At last a slow drum-beat in the distance announced the coming of the flag-draped corpse, its face now like that of a marble statue wearing an unforgettable expression of determination and courage which Jawaharlal's mercurial changes of countenance had obscured in life. There was a small bustle round the pyre on the raised funeral platform, where piles of sandalwood had been stacked as they were stacked for Gandhi three hundred yards away sixteen years ago. Six officer pall-bearers lifted the body on to the pyre and an ochre-clad priest laid sticks of sandalwood round it. The national flag, which must not be burned, was removed, and the corpse, wrapped in a white sheet, gradually disappeared under a pile of sandalwood, flower petals and silken scarves.

Then, shortly after half-past four, came the moment when Jawaharlal's teenage grandson Sanjay crossed the dead Prime Minister's hands, tore the winding-sheet, and put a match to the camphor-soaked wood. Indira's younger son—'a fair-skinned handsome boy who could be any teenager from Europe or America', one journalist wrote—had been brought from a holiday in Kashmir for this grim purpose: his elder

L*

164 *Envoy Extraordinary*

brother, at college in England, could not arrive in time. Round the pyre the chanting of the priests, which had continued for hours, went steadily on: 'Let your eye go to the sun, your life to the wind, turn to the waters if they draw you, rest in the green plants.'

The pyre caught fire with a sudden blaze, and a great cry came from the multitude as the black smoke climbed towards the sky. The soaked wood burned more fiercely as devout hands anointed it with perfumed *samagri*, a mixture of sandalwood, sawdust, and incense. Bugles played 'The Last Post', followed as in England by a rifle salute.

'It is unbelievable,' wrote Anne Sharpley, 'that the lovely grey ghost that we saw handed in a bier up the steps to the pyre beside the Jumna river should be under those flames and casually stacked logs.'

As the heat became fiercer, the closest mourners stepped from the plinth. Vijaya Lakshmi had already moved down. Shaking off friends who endeavoured to restrain her, and murmuring with her hands to her head: 'No, I can't!' she pushed her way blindly towards the steps and joined the anonymous crowds.

Her brother, she knew, had not wanted these Hindu religious rites. In his Will, dated June 21, 1954, he had recorded his gratitude for the affection shown him by the people of India, and then continued: 'I wish to declare with all earnestness that I do not want any religious cere- monies performed for me after my death. I do not believe in any such ceremonies, and to submit to them even as a matter of form would be hypocrisy, and an attempt to delude ourselves and others.'

Parts of that Will were to be read over the radio by Vijaya Lakshmi on June 3rd; her words, reported *The Times* correspondent, 'came like his voice at the prime of his life, strong, lyrical when speaking of his beloved India, but rejecting sternly "the shackles of religion and tradition that bind and constrain her and divide her people, and sup- press vast numbers of them".' He had requested cremation, and asked that a handful of his ashes should be thrown into the Ganges, but in this, he insisted, there was no religious significance. He had known the Ganges and Jumna rivers since his boyhood and loved them through his life.

'The Ganges especially is the river of India, beloved of her people, round which are intertwined her racial memories, her hopes and fears, her songs of triumph. She has been a symbol of India's age-long culture and civilization, ever-changing, ever-flowing, and yet ever the same. She reminds me of the snow-covered peaks and the deep valleys of the Himalayas which I have loved so much and of the vast plains below where my life and work have been cast.'

## Nightfall on the Jumna
165

Vijaya Lakshmi went on to tell her hearers of his final wish. He had asked that the remainder of his ashes should be carried high in an aircraft and scattered 'over the fields where the peasants of India toil, so that they might mingle with the dust and soil of India and become an indistinguishable part of her'.

Perhaps, owing to the swift mind that they shared and their characteristic impatience with fools and sycophants, Vijaya Lakshmi, alone of them all, had really understood him, for his wishes had been disregarded. Now, as the early tropical twilight approached, the undesired rites were almost over. Sheik Abdullah of Kashmir, in a final gesture— was it of forgiveness or renunciation?—threw *samagri* on to the pyre. The now faceless crowd of white figures stretching to the horizon, their robes crumpled and wet with heat, could see the flames rise heavenward and then diminish. They did not move even when a sudden dust-storm arose, temporarily blotting out the sky. Reverent hands stripped the funeral carriage clean of its decorations. After a life-time of service to India, Jawaharlal Nehru, whose mortal remains it had borne, was finally, inexorably, gone.

The fire died down in the blue-grey Indian dusk, leaving only a glowing golden coronet like an immortal flower. On the foundations that Jawaharlal and his family had built, a new India would arise, illumined by the unquenchable radiance of his vision. Not least among the creators of those foundations had been Vijaya Lakshmi Pandit.

Before her and before all India, a gigantic question mark, lay the uncertain future with its challenge.

EPILOGUE

# The Torch-Bearer

———◆◆◆———

'I pray ... that he should know there are many hands to carry
forward the torch he now bears.'
Vijaya Lakshmi Pandit, *The Family Bond,* op. cit.

WITHIN six months, laying aside her grief, Vijaya Lakshmi had
accepted the future's challenge in a fashion that perhaps she alone could
have achieved.

She had been unable to witness the actual destruction of her brother's
body, and the following day had wept when Anne Sharpley spoke to
her, but tears were not her normal response to tragedy. However
painful the inner wound, they were soon overcome.

From the time that she had reluctantly accepted the decorative but
undynamic position of State Governor, she had persisted despite official
discouragement in looking for more active political work. The customary argument that its rough-and-tumble was less dignified than
that of a conspicuous figurehead had left her unmoved.

Jawaharlal's death, and the fact that his constituency was now
vacant, renewed her determination. Nowhere, she knew, could she
serve her brother's memory and carry on his ideals so effectively as in
the national Parliament. Undeterred by previous resistance, she asked
if she could be the Congress Candidate for the forthcoming by-election
at Phulpur, sixteen miles from Allahabad. It had not only been Jawaharlal's constituency for seventeen years, but was a key seat in the
United Provinces.

This constituency had been understandably offered to Indira, who
with her customary distaste for controversial politics had declined it.
Vijaya Lakshmi was now told that the contest would be very difficult;
that the Nehru influence was on the wane in the United Provinces, their
former stronghold; that her defeat would seriously damage the prestige
of the Congress Party, and would mean her own political eclipse; that
the United Socialist Party under Mr Soligram Jaiswal, by far the

## The Torch-bearer 167

strongest of the three Opposition candidates, would be very hard to beat.

She only said: 'Freedom is not for the timid. If one wishes to be in politics, one must be ready to face all eventualities.' Finally, supported by the new Prime Minister, Mr Shastri, who broke with precedent to help her in the by-election, she was nominated for the seat, and staked her reputation on the result.

She took in her stride two important engagements made for her many months earlier in Oxford, where she had agreed to open a new house for graduates at Somerville College. The University proposed on this occasion to confer on her an Honorary Doctorate, an award which even her brother had not received from Oxford. With her own by-election impending in late November, she flew to England three days before the British General Election of 1964; spent Election day, which incongruously clashed with the Degree-giving, at Oxford; and returned to India the same evening after an official dinner at Somerville. The College, to show its appreciation, awarded her an Honorary Fellowship.

During November her hard-fought campaign involved huge election meetings attended by persistent crowds, in which many of the women wept for Jawaharlal's memory. She campaigned with a Gandhi-like humility which few voters had expected from a former Ambassador, touring the villages on foot while her opponents travelled round in a car preceded by a motor-cyclist with a flag, and spending the last twenty-five days of the contest living in a tent amid the peasant electors.[1] Nevertheless *The Scotsman's* Special Correspondent, Mr Ashwini Kumari, laconically reported: 'The harsh facts of economic life seem to be against her.'

On November 22nd the polling took place. Two days later, the world's Press announced her decisive victory. She had won by a majority of 58,000 votes over the formidable Mr Jaiswal.[2]

Henceforth, a woman enriched by incomparable experience, her beauty transformed but undiminished, she would bring to a new and constructive purpose the inspiration of the 'fiery girl' who had raised

---

*Time*, December 4, 1964.

[2] A paragraph in my letter to her on May 28th had proved to be prophetic: 'You will, I know, continue to play your own part in the struggle. When your husband died, Gandhiji wrote you that you would find "courage in yourself". You found it, and being what you are you will find it again. You have many years of work for India before you, and those of us here who care for you pray that the strength and opportunity to do it will be yours. Your brother could have no better memorial than your further fulfilment of the confidence which Gandhi reposed in you both.'

168 *Envoy Extraordinary*

the voice of revolutionary India outside the Conference Hall at San Francisco two decades ago.

With her victory in the Phulpur by-election, she had lifted her brother's torch from his ashes and held it aloft. No longer an 'Envoy Extraordinary' operating in the chief foreign capitals of the world, she had become a leading politician carrying on, in her own country and his own constituency, Jawaharlal Nehru's work for the building of modern India.

# APPENDIX

### CHIEF BOOKS AND DOCUMENTS CONSULTED

Jawaharlal Nehru. *An Autobiography*. London, John Lane, 1936.

*Ed.* Shyam Kumari Nehru. *Our Cause. A Symposium of Indian Women.* Allahabad, Kitabistan, Circ. 1936.

Vijaya Lakshmi Pandit. *So I Became a Minister.* Circ. 1938.

Krishna Nehru Hutheesing. *With No Regrets.* Bombay, Padma Publications, Ltd., 1944.

Padmini Sen Gupta. *Pioneer Women of India.* Bombay, Thacker & Co., 1944.

Vijaya Lakshmi Pandit. *Prison Days.* Calcutta, Signet Press, 1946 (Third Edition).

Jawaharlal Nehru. *The Discovery of India.* Calcutta, 1946.

Nayantara Sahgal. *Prison and Chocolate Cake.* London, Gollancz, 1954.

*Ed.* Tara Ali Baig. *Women of India.* (Under the auspices of the National Council of Women in India.) Publications Division, Ministry of Information and Broadcasting, Government of India Press, 1958.

Michael Brecher. *Nehru, a Political Biography.* Oxford University Press, 1959.

*Ed.* Rafiq Zakaria. *A Study of Nehru.* Foreword by Rajendra Prasad, Times of India Press, 1959.

*Ed.* J. N. Chakrabartti. *Dr. Syud Hossain.* Calcutta, P. Ghosh & Co., 1960.

*Ed.* Vera Brittain and G. Handley-Taylor. *Selected Letters of Winifred Holtby and Vera Brittain.* London, Brown, 1960.

Jawaharlal Nehru. *India's Foreign Policy.* (Speeches 1946–61.) Publications Division, Government of India, 1961.

Nayantara Sahgal. *From Fear Set Free.* London, Gollancz, 1962.

B. R. Nanda. *The Nehrus. Motilal and Jawaharlal.* London, Allen & Unwin, Ltd., 1962.

*Introd.* Krishna Nehru Hutheesing. *Nehru's Letters to his Sister.* London, Faber, 1963.

Ian Stephens. *Pakistan.* London, Ernest Benn, 1963.

*The Constitution of India,* as modified up to March 1, 1963.

T. J. S. George. *Krishna Menon. A Biography.* London, Cape, 1964.

India, Annual Reviews. Information Service of India, India House, London.

170        *Envoy Extraordinary*

Occasional Correspondence between Mrs Pandit and the Author, 1951–64.

PAMPHLETS

M. C. Chagla. (Ambassador of India to the USA, 1958-61.) *Our Two Countries* (collected speeches). Information Service of India, Washington, DC, 1961.

Dr Sarvepalli Radhakrishnan, President of India. Speeches collected during a nine-day State visit to the USA. Embassy of India, Washington, DC, 1963.

B. K. Nehru. (Ambassador of India to the USA.) *Speaking of India.* Information Service of India, Washington, DC, 1963.

Women's Council, London. *The Rôle of Women in Asia To-day*, 1963.

AUTHOR'S NOTE

Innumerable ephemeral articles on Mrs Pandit, of which I have read a large number, have appeared in newspapers and magazines throughout the English-speaking world and in India, but more permanent studies are few. I have nevertheless deliberately refrained from reading a recent American biography, *Madame Ambassador*, by Anne Guthrie, owing to the risk of subconscious plagiarism.

# INDEX

## A

Abdullah, Sheik, 158, 165
Acheson, Dean, 100, 113
Adenauer, Konrad, 149
Al Mussawar (Egypt), 114
Aleman, President Miguel (of Mexico), 104
Allahabad Municipal Board, 47
Alexander, A. V. (later Earl), 52, 75
All-India Congress Committee, 159
All-India Women's Conference, 15, 17, 22, 41, 47, 53
Altrincham, Lord (John Grigg), 146
Amery, Rt. Hon. Leo, 15, 52, 74
*Amrita Bazar Patrika*, 66
Amritsar (massacre), 26, 33, 34, 36, 43, 44, 82
Anand Bhawan (later Swaraj Bhawan), 23, 31–2, 34, 35, 40, 41, 42, 45, 46, 51, 55, 56, 57, 82, 108
*Apartheid* (South Africa), 76, 78, 79, 80, 153, 157
Ashby, Mrs Corbett, 15, 22
Atlantic Charter, 67
Attlee, C. R. (Prime Minister), 52, 74, 100 n., 137
*Autobiography* (Nehru), 54, 56, 56 n.
Azad, Maulana, 74, 132

## B

Bacon, Francis, 55
Badawi, M., 115
Bajpai, U. S., 9
Bandaranike, Mrs (Ceylon), 163
Bandung Conference, 122, 129
Banks, Sir John G. (Lord Provost), 130
Bareilly (prison), 60, 73
Bell, Gertrude, 16
Bernardino, Miss Minerva, 116
Besant, Annie, 44
Bevan, Aneurin, 131, 136
Bevin, Ernest, 78
Bharat Welfare League, 72
Bhave, Vinoba, 29
Bibi Anima, 35
Bikaner, Maharajah of, 143
Biography (types of), 12–13
Bolshoi Theatre, 91
Bolton, Mrs Frances (USA), 116
Bondfield, Rt. Hon. Margaret, 22, 49 n.

Bose, Sir J., 23
Bose, Subhas, 75
Bowles, Chester, 111
Brandeis University, Mass., 153
Brecher, Michael, 60 n., 86, 86 n.
Bright, Richard, 10
Brittain, Vera, 22
Bromfield, Louis, 70
Brown, George, 162
Buck, Pearl, 70
Buddha, The, 95, 130
Buddha, Year of the, 128
Buddhi (Indian cook), 125
Bunyan, John, 12
Burch, Stanley (*News Chronicle*), 47

## C

Cadbury, Elizabeth, 22
Catlin, Professor George, 10, 72
Chakravarti, Amiya, 42
Chiang Kai-Shek, Madame, 58, 65
Chinese invasion (1962), 105 n., 110, 111
Chou En-Lai, 109, 147, 161 n.
*Christian Science Monitor*, 97, 109, 116
Churchill, Winston, 11, 120, 121, 128
Colby, Ruth Gage, 9
Community Development Movement, 143
Congressman Celler, 70
Congressman Coffee, 70
*Constitution of the Republic of India*, 99, 99 n., 151 n.
Cordier, Andrew, 119
Courtney, Kathleen, 22
Cripps Mission, 26
Cripps, Sir Stafford, 23, 52, 53, 72, 72 n., 75, 127
Curzon, Lord, 32

## D

*Daily Telegraph*, 85
Dandi, pilgrimage to, 26
Das, C. R., 44
Declaration of Independence, 99
Desai, Mahadev, 25
Desai, M. J. (Acting High Commissioner), 110
*Discovery of India, The* (Nehru), 64
Doren, Irita van 66
Douglas-Home, Sir Alec, 162

# 172

## Index

Dulles, J. F., 118; plan *re* Suez, 129–30
Durgi, 24
Dyer, General, 34

### E

Eden, Anthony, 121, 128, 131, 132
Eisenhower, President D., 118
Elizabeth, Queen, 137
Emmet, Mrs Evelyn, 112, 116
*Encyclopaedia Britannica*, 114
Erhard, Dr Ludwig, 149
Evans, Sir Ifor, 127
*Evening Standard*, 146, 161 n., 163

### F

*Family Bond, The* (V. L. Pandit), 166
Fawcett Library, 10
Feisal, Emir, 78, 113
*Foreign Affairs* (India), 148
Formosa, 122, 148 n.
Foyle, Christina, 10, 138; Foyle's Luncheon, 137, 139
Franco, General, 135
Frankfurt, Treaty of, 111 n.
Franks, Sir Oliver (later Lord), 96, 107
*From Fear Set Free* (N. Sahgal), 90, 92, 103, 108, 124
Frost, Robert, 109
Fry, Margery, 22
Fu, Dr (Chinese Ambassador to Moscow), 91

### G

Gaitskell, Hugh, 127
Gandhi, Devadas, 133
Gandhi, Feroze, 23, 40, 42, 136
Gandhi–Irwin Agreement (1931), 27, 53
Gandhi, Kasturba, 37, 41
Gandhi, Mahatma, 11, 14, 16, 17, 23, 24, 25, 26, 27, 28, 29, 33, 34, 35, 37, 39, 41, 43, 44, 45, 47, 49, 52, 53, 57, 62, 64, 65, 67, 74, 75, 76, 77, 79, 83, 84, 85, 92, 93, 95, 114, 137, 146, 156, 161 n., 162, 163, 167 n.
Gandhi, Manilal, 76–7
Gandhi, Rajiv, 144
Gandhi, Sanjay, 144, 163
Gandreth, Major-General, K. P., 145 n.
Ganju, J. N., 9
George V, 137, 163
George VI, 137
George, T. J. S., 101 n., 113, 145 n.
Gestapo List, 15
Goa, 84, 128, 144–6, 145 n.
Gopal, Ram, 130

Gore-Booth, Sir Paul, 162
Government of India Act (1935), 48
'Great Calcutta Killing', 76
*Guardian* (*Manchester*), 86 n., 92, 146, 146 n.
Gujerat (New State), 136, 150
Gundevia, Y. D., 120
Gunther, Frances, 59
Gupta, N. N., 9
Gupta, Rabindranath, 9, 161

### H

Halifax, Lord, 71
Halliday, Edward, 10
Hammarskjoeld, Dag, 113, 114, 141–2, 148
Han-Fu, Chang, 147
Hardinge, Lord (Viceroy), 77
Harldwar (cholera epidemic), 49
Harrison, Agatha, 15, 22, 63, 120–1
Harrison, Irene, 10, 162
Hawes, Elizabeth, 66
*Herald Tribune* (N.Y.), 66, 162
Hindu Succession Bill, 132
*Hindustan Standard*, 67
*Hindustani Times*, 87, 133
Holtby, Winifred, 13, 77
Home, Lord (Foreign Secretary), 126–7
Hornaday, Mary (*Christian Science Monitor*), 116
Hossain, Dr Syud, 66, 72, 73, 93
Hungarian revolt, 122, 131–2
Hutheesing, Raja, 29, 40, 42

### I

Ikramullah, Begum Shaista, 10
India House (Düsseldorf), 149
India House (London), 12, 96, 124–5, 131, 161
Indian Council for Child Welfare, 48 n.
*Indian Opinion*, 76–7
'Indian Plan' (on Korea), 112
*India's Foreign Policy* (Nehru's speeches), 87, 145 n., 148 n.
Indo-China, 122
Information, Central Office of, 10
International Co-operation Year, 155–6

### J

Jaipur, Maharanee of, 143
Jaiswal, Soligram (United Socialist Party), 166–7
Japanese Peace Treaty, 101–2
Jefferson, Thomas, 99 n.
Jinnah, Mohammed Ali, 43, 73, 74
Juliana, Queen, 133

# Index

173

## K

Kabadi, Sunder, 9, 146
Kabir, Hon. Hamayun, 9
Kalidasa, 56
Karikal, 128
Kaul, Raj, 32
Kaur, Rajkumari Amrit, 17, 28, 158
Kennedy, Ludovic, 10, 35, 37, 46, 55, 92, 105, 106–7, 123
Kennedy, President, J. F., 156
Kensington Palace Gardens (Indian Residency), 124–5
Khali (Pandit summer home), 40, 61, 73
Khan, Begum Liaquat Ali, 112
Khan, Liaquat Ali, 86
Kher, B. G., 87, 100 n., 124
Khrushchev, N., 89
Korean War, 102, 102 n., 104, 105 n., 110, 111, 113, 117, 122
Kripalani, Acharya, 75, 145, 166
Krishnamachari, T. T., 158
Kuisevitsky, Serge, 88
Kumari, Ashwini (*Scotsman*), 167

## L

*Ladies' Home Journal*, 37, 101 n.
Layton, Dorothea, 22
League of Nations, 77 n., 77, 117
Lee, Jennie, 136
Leger, Fernand, 117
Lenin, 11
Lester, Muriel, 34, 52
*Let My People Go* (Luthuli), 157
Lie, Trygve, 113
Lloyd, Rt. Hon. Selwyn, 120, 129
Lodge, Richard, 115, 118
Luebe, President Heinrich, 149
Luthuli, Chief Albert, 157

## M

Macmillan, Rt. Hon. Harold, 121, 132, 133–4
Maharashtra, 136, 149, 150–2
Mahe, 128
Malan, Dr D. (South Africa), 79
Malaviya, Pandit Madan Mohan, 31, 45, 54
Malik, Jacob, 111, 115, 118, 126
*Man and Superman* (Shaw), 159
*Man of Two Worlds* (broadcast), 54
Manu, 16
Manuilsky, D. Z. (Ukrainia), 78
McNeil, Hector, 114

Mears, Sir Grimwood, 33
Mehta, Mrs Hansa, 17
Mehta, H. E. Dr Jivraj, 10, 162
Menon, Krishna, 100–1, 101 n., 112, 113, 114, 119, 122, 124, 128, 129, 131, 145, 146, 147, 148, 152
Menon, Mrs Lakshmi, 17, 114, 116
Mikoyan, A., 89
Mills, Mrs Ogden Livingston, 69
Minto, Lord (Viceroy), 77
Molotov, V. L., 86, 89
Moraes, Dom, 146
Moraes, Frank, 146
Morton Eleanor (*Women Behind Mahatma Gandhi*), 43
'Mother of the Year' Award, 103
Mountbatten, Edwina (Lady), 127, 135
Mountbatten, Lord (Louis), 81, 127, 135, 162
Mountbatten, Pamela, 162
Mulchrone, Vincent (*Daily Mail*), 10
Mundaliar, Sir Ramaswarmi, 68

## N

Naidu, Padmaja, 17, 147
Naidu, Sarojini, 17, 34, 43, 82, 93, 147, 158 n.
Nanda, G. L., 158, 160
Nasser, President, 128, 129
National Committee for Indian Freedom (USA), 66, 70
*Nehru: A Political Biography* (Brecher), 60 n., 61 n.
Nehru, B. K. (Indian Ambassador to Washington), 83 n.
Nehru, Indira (Mrs Gandhi), 23, 24, 28, 40–1, 44, 47, 135–6, 144, 158, 160, 163, 166
Nehru, Jawaharlal
    Domination of Nehru dynasty in India ended by his death, 11
    His part in shaping the Commonwealth, 11
    Response to idea of Mrs Pandit's biography, 9, 12
    BBC programme on him, 10, 31, 32, 36, 42
    Letter to Krishna, 22
    Reading and writing in prison, 25
    Congress President (1929), 26, 44
    Arrested 1931, 27
    Sentenced to four years' imprisonment, 29, 53
    Origins of family, 32

# Index

Nehru, Jawaharlal—*continued*
Pledges himself to national movement, 34
Education, 36
Friendship with Ranjit Pandit, 39
Daughter's marriage, 40–1
Sentenced to six months' imprisonment, 44
Visit to Switzerland, 44
Death of his father Motilal, 45
Refuses to support Second World War, 52
Refuses suggestions from Cripps Mission, 53
In prison with Ranjit Pandit, 54
Agrees to education of his nieces in U.S.A., 58
Reactions to Ranjit's death, 63
Grief over Bengal famine, 64
Freed from prison by British Labour Government, 72
Holiday in Kashmir, 74
Convenes Constituent Assembly as President of Congress, 75
Faces communal civil war, 76
Heads Interim Government, 81
Becomes Prime Minister of India, 82
Defines policy of non-alignment, 83–4
Defines his policy towards Communism, 85
States intentions on women diplomats, 86
Appoints Mrs Pandit as Ambassador to Moscow, 86
Alone after death of Gandhi, 93
Accepts invitation to visit USA, 96
Visits USA, 99–100
Influenced by Krishna Menon, 100–1
Complex relationship with Mrs Pandit, 101
Outlines policy towards USA, 101
Praises his Ambassadors, 103
Fights the General Election of 1952, 109
Deplores the world's attitude to China, 110
Disillusionment with China's policy, 111
Appeals for ban on nuclear weapons, 119
Visits President Tito, 120
Attends Commonwealth Prime Ministers' Conference, 124
Attempt on his life, 127
Visits Ireland, 128
Pronouncement on Goa, 128

Visits Nasser and signs treaty of friendship with Egypt, 129
Condemns Suez dispute, 129
Denounces Anglo-French aggression, 130
Faces Hungarian crisis, 131
Decides to keep India in Commonwealth, 133
Visits Holland, 133
Welcomes Harold Macmillan to Delhi, 134
Eases communal tension helped by Lady Mountbatten, 135
Visits Aneurin Bevan and Jennie Lee, 136
Portrait painted for India House, 137
Health begins to fail, 144
Authorizes seizure of Goa, 145
Goes to England for medical treatment, 147
Holds banquet for Chou En-lai (1960), 147
Declares state of emergency after Chinese invasion, 148
Appoints Mrs Pandit Governor of Maharashtra, 149
Makes her leader of Indian delegation to UN Eighteenth Assembly, 152
Proposes International Cooperation Year, 156
Celebrates 74th birthday, 157
Growing ill-health, 157–8
Receives Sheik Abdullah, 158
Visits Dehra Dun, 158
Visits Nepal and Bombay, 159
Second stroke and death, 160
Funeral procession and cremation, 160–4
Will read by Mrs Pandit, 164–5
Nehru, Krishna (Hutheesing), 21, 22, 27, 29, 32, 35, 37, 40, 42, 43, 45, 47, 51, 54, 57, 58, 59, 63, 101, 101 n., 163
Nehru, Motilal, 17, 26, 37, 31–8, 41, 43, 44 (death of), 45, 47, 51, 138
Nehru, Swarup Kumari (later Vijaya Lakshmi Pandit), 29, 31–8, 43
Nehru, Swarup Rani (wife of Motilal), 35, 47, 51
*New York Post*, 52, 69
*New York Times*, 95, 96, 152
Nichols, Beverley, 66
Nicholls, Heaton, 78
Nkrumah, Kwame, 134
Noon, Sir Firoz Khan, 68

# Index

175

## O

Oberai, Col, G. R., I.M.S., 61
Observer, The, 161 n.
O'Ceallaigh, Mr Sean T., President of Eire, 127
O'Donovan, Patrick, 54
Onlooker (Bombay), 17
Orusholdt, Anna, 23
Oxford Mail & Times, 10

## P

Padma Vibhushan Award, 146
Pakistan (Ian Stephens), 82 n.
Panchayat Raj Bill (U.P.), 49, Ref. to, 100, 143
Panchsheel Agreement, 147
Pandit, Chandalekha, 'Lecky', (Mrs Mehta), 9, 23, 24, 27–8, 45, 46, 55, 57, 58, 59, 62, 65, 73, 88, 91, 95, 103
Pandit, Nayantara (Mrs Sahgal), 9, 24, 34, 35, 39, 45, 46, 53, 55, 57, 58, 59, 62–3, 72, 77, 79, 82, 88, 90, 91, 92, 103, 104, 108, 109, 123, 124, 125
Pandit, Ranjit Sitaram, 29, 37, 38–42, 44, 45, 48–9, 53, 54, 55, 56, 57, 58–9, 60–1, 62–3
Pandit, Rita Vitasta (Mrs Dar), 9, 23, 24, 45, 46, 55, 56, 62, 65, 77, 96, 142
Pandit, Vijaya Lakshmi
  Her part in India's story altered by death of her brother, 11
  Unique share in diplomacy of the new India, 11
  Her co-operation in creation of this biography, 12
  More a pacemaker than a woman or an Indian, 13
  Shares two formative experiences with the author, 14
  Her Punch article on position of Indian women, 15
  Share in founding of All-India Women's Conference, 17, 45, 53
  Her debt to Sarojini Naidu, 17
  Her long series of key positions, 17
  The burden of her inheritance, 17–18
  Hospitality and generosity to author, 18
  Her capacity for objective judgment, 19
  Her creation of a new image of the modern Indian woman, 19
  Experiences as a prisoner of the British, 21–30
  Protest by British women after her second arrest (1940), 22

  Birth, family, childhood and youth, 30–6
  Meeting and marrying Ranjit Pandit, 36–40
  Her wedding, 41
  Joins freedom movement and settles in Allahabad, 42
  First contacts with Gandhi, 43–5
  Death of her father Motilal, 45
  Birth of her three daughters, 45
  Interview with Ludovic Kennedy (1961), 46, 55, 105, 106, 123
  Relations with her daughters, 46
  Contacts with Kamala Nehru (wife of Jawaharlal), 47
  Chairman of Allahabad Municipal Board, 47–8
  Election as Congress candidate in United Provinces, 48–9
  Minister of Local Self-Government and Public Health in the U.P., 49–51
  Death of her mother, 51
  Resigns from Provincial Ministry (1939), 52
  Reactions to Jawaharlal's severe prison sentence, 53–4
  Her third prison period, 53–61
  Anxiety for Ranjit after his arrest, 55–6
  Concern for Jawaharlal, 56–7
  Decision to send daughters to America, 57–8
  Parting with daughters and their experiences, 58–60
  Failure of Ranjit's health after transfer to Bareilly Prison, 60–1
  Death of Ranjit, 61
  Support of Gandhi and her daughters, 62–3
  Letter to Agatha Harrison, 63
  Service in Bengal famine, 64
  Threat of penury after death of Ranjit, 64–5
  Decision to go to America with help of Americans, 65
  Organisation of lecture platforms for her by the National Committee for Indian Freedom (USA), 66–8
  Her arrival in San Francisco (1945) as representative of independent India, 68–71
  Visit to Sacramento Valley, 71–2
  Post-war apartment with daughters in New York, 72–3

# 176 Index

Pandit, Vijaya Lakshmi—*continued*
Return to India to take up her U.P. Portfolio, 73
Changes in India after advent of British Labour Government, 74–6
First official mission as leader of Indian delegation to United Nations, 76–80
Adoption of her resolution on South Africa, 78–80
Poem to her by Edith Lovejoy Pierce, 81
Return to India as Congress Minister, 81
Appointment to Indian Embassy in Moscow as India's first Ambassador, 82, 86
Independent India's diplomatic objectives, 82–5
Experiences at Indian Embassy in Moscow, 87–93
Second and third visits to UN, 88–9
Problems of a woman Ambassador, 91–2
Her grief for the deaths of Gandhi, Sarojini Naidu, and Syud Hossain, 92–4
Appointment as Indian Ambassador to Washington (1949), 94–6
Experiences in Washington, 96–107
Her brother's visit to USA, 99–100
Friendship with Mr Dean Acheson, 100
Her relations with Krishna Menon, 100–1
Problems of Indo-American diplomacy, 101–2
Korean War, 102
Wheat Loan negotiations, 102–3
Visit of her daughters to USA, 103–4
'Mother of the Year' Luncheon and Honorary Degrees, 103–4
Ambassador to Mexico, 104–5
Contrasts between Moscow and Washington, 105–7
Return to India for General Election, 107
India's General Election of 1952, 108–9
Her election by large majority, 109
Visit to China, March 1952, 109–11
Conclusion of Korean War, 111–13
Leadership of Indian Delegation to Seventh Assembly of UN, 112–13
Election as President of UN Eighth Assembly, 113

Her work as UN President, 113–19
Description of UN Headquarters, 116–17
Travels in Asia and Europe, 119–21
Withdrawal of India's diplomatic mission to South Africa, 120
Appointment in 1954 as India's High Commissioner to UK, 121
Diplomatic relationships 1954–6, 122–3
Transformed relations between Indians and British, 123
The London Residency (9 Kensington Palace Gardens), 124–5
Speaking and travelling engagements, 125–33
Visit to Dublin (1955), 127
Honorary Degrees, 127
Reception for Indian President, 128
Suez Crisis, 128–31
Hungarian revolt, 131
Second Visit to Ireland (1957), 131
India's Second Election (1957), 132
Comments on special qualities of women, 132
Visit to Northern Ireland (April 1957), 132–3
Welcomes brother to Commonwealth Prime Ministers' Conference, 133
Accompanies brother to Holland, 133
Visit to San Francisco for UNESCO Conference, 133
Accompanies Harold Macmillan on visit to Delhi, 134
Visit to Ghana, 134
Appointed first Indian Ambassador to Spain, 135
Visit to Germany to receive Dorothy Schlozer Medal, 135
Tribute to Lady Mountbatten (1960), 135
Speech at 75th birthday of Mrs Roosevelt, 136
Visit with Jawaharlal to Aneurin Bevan and Jennie Lee, 136
Accompanies Queen Elizabeth on her 1961 visit to India, 137
Her portrait painted and presented to her brother (March 1961), 137
Farewell speech at Foyle's Luncheon, 137–8
Failure of health through overwork, 138
Relinquishes post, 139
Her success as High Commissioner, 139–40

# Index 177

Pandit, Vijaya Lakshmi—*continued*
Visits Sweden for funeral of Dag Hammarskjoeld, 141
Illness in Greece, 142
Takes flat in Bombay, 142
Her comparisons between India in 1947 and in 1961, 142–4
Changes in her relatives, 144
Anxiety over seizure of Goa, 144–6
Sees India's third General Election, 146
Receives the Padma Vibhushan award, 146–7
Experiences the Chinese invasion of 1962, 147–8
Opens International Hall of Residence in London, 148
Founds a new India House in Düsseldorf, 149
Appointed Governor of Maharashtra, 149
Occupies Raj Bhawan on Malabar Hill, 150
Work of a State Governor, 151–2
Leads India's delegation to the 18th Assembly of the UN, 152
Revisits Ghana, 152
Criticizes Pakistan at the UN, 152–3
Pleads for a total Test-Ban Treaty, 154
Pays tribute to Mrs Roosevelt (1963), on first anniversary of her death, 155
Attends funeral of President Kennedy, and speaks at a UN Memorial Meeting, 156
Appeals to world's trading countries to boycott South Africa, 157
Returns to India to find her brother gravely ill, 157
Hastens from Bombay after his second stroke (May 26), but arrives too late to see him alive, 160
Letter to the author on his death, 160–1
Attends his funeral, 161–4
Reads his Will over the radio, 164–5
Determines to fight the by-election at Phalpur, his constituency, 166–7
Visits Oxford to open the Somerville Graduate House and receive an Honorary Degree, 167
Wins the election (November 2, 1964) by a majority of 58,000 votes, 167
Changes from envoy into a leading politician, 168
Panikkar, Sardar K. H., 158
Pankhurst, Sylvia, 136

Panmunjom, 111, 112
Pant, Pandit Govind, 49
Parkes, Mrs Noreen, 10
Patel, Nanalal, 72
Patel, Sardar, 75
Pearson, Lester, 113, 117
*People's Voice, The*, 81
Pethick-Lawrence, Emmeline, 22
Pethick-Lawrence, F. W. (Lord), 13, 29, 52, 72, 74, 75, 127, 133, 137
Phalpur (Allahabad), 150, 166–7, 168
Philip, Prince, 137
Phoenix, Natal (Gandhian Settlement), 76
Pierce, Edith Lovejoy, 81
Prasad, President Rajendra, 137, 147
*Prison and Chocolate Cake* (N. Sangal), 34a, 57, 62
*Prison Days* (V. L. Pandit), 55, 60
Pondicherry, 128
*Punch*, 15

## Q
'Quit India' Resolution, 23, 26, 27

## R
Radhakrishnan, Sir Sarvepalli, 128, 147, 156
Raghavan, N., 147
Raj Bhawan (Governor's House in Bombay), 12, 50, 150–1
Rajagopalachari, C., 146
Rama Rau, Sir Benegal, 96
Ranganadhan, Sir S., 149
*Reynolds' News*, 112–13
Ribaud, Marc (*Sunday Times*), 10
Ripley, Josephine (*Christian Science Monitor*), 97
Romanis, Mr Hugo, 36
Romulo, General, 113
Roosevelt, Eleanor, 60, 67, 88, 99, 114, 115, 117, 125, 136, 155
Roosevelt, President F. D., 69
Rowlett Acts, 43, 43 n.
Roy, Simon (*Daily Mail*), 10
Royden, Maude, 22
Russell, Bertrand, 143

## S
Sabarmati (ashram), 37
Sabbaroyan, Dr P., 149
Sahgal, Gautam, 103
San Francisco Conference, 68–72, 76, 78, 89, 95, 168

# 178       *Index*

Sapru, P. N., 62
Sapru, Sir Tej Bahadur, 31, 62
Schlozer, Dorothy (Medal), 135
*Scotsman, The,* 106 n., 167
Sekaninova-Cakrtoya, Dr Gertruda, 112
*Selected Letters of Winifred Holtby and Vera Brittain,* 77 n.
Sen, Ela (*Housewife*), 115
Sharpley, Anne (*Evening Standard*), 10, 161 n., 163, 164, 166
Shastri, Lal Bahadur, 158, 167
Shaw, G. Bernard, 159
Sheth, Amritlal D., 70
Shivernik, Nikolai, 87
Shridharani, Dr Krishnalal, 73
Silverstone, Marilyn (*Sunday Times*), 10
Simon Commission, 44
Singh, Dr Anup, 73
Singh, Iqbal (*Illustrated Weekly of India*), 79, 97, 113
Singh, H. E. the Hon. Kewal, 9
Skrzesezewski, Stanislaw, 113
Smuts, Field-Marshal Jan, 77, 78–80
*So I Became a Minister* (V. L. Pandit), 49–50
Somerville College, Oxford, 167
Sorensen, Reginald (later Lord), 138
South Africa, 76–80, 86, 88, 92, 120, 153, 157
Spaak, P-H. (Belgium), 77
*Speaking of India* (B. K. Nehru), 83 n.
Srivastava, Lady, 48
Stacey, Tom (*Sunday Times*), 10, 157, 162
Stalin, J., 85, 87, 89, 98
Stephens, Ian, 82 n.
Stevenson, Hon. Adlai, 9
Stowe, Leland, 66
Stratemeyer, General, 65
Streat, Sir Raymond, 126
Strydom, Dr (South Africa), 79
Subramaniam, C., 160
Success, Lake, 95
Suez crisis, 122, 129–32, 139
Summerskill, Dr Edith (later Baroness), 22, 131
*Sunday Times,* 10, 157, 161 n., 162
Swatantra Party, 146

### T

Tagore, Rabindranath, 32, 147; centenary, 137–8
*Testament of Experience,* 69 n.
*Testament of Friendship,* 13

Test-Ban Treaty, 154
Thimayya, Lt.-General, 112
Thorndike, Sybil, 22
*Time* (USA), 167 n
*Times, The,* 146, 158, 161 n., 162, 164
Tito, President, 120
Truman, President, 96, 100
Trumbull, Robert (*New York Times*), 95 106 n.

### U

Unesco, 133
United Nations, 9, 11, 36, 72, 76, 76 n., 77, 78–80, 79 n., 87, 88–9, 92, 100, 102, 104, 110, 113–19, 131, 137, 139, 141, 146, 152–7
*Unity of India, The* (Nehru), 75

### V

Van Balluseck, 115
Vedas, The, 15
Verwoerd, Dr (South Africa), 79
'Vicky', 161 n.
Vietnam, 121
Vishinsky, Andrei, 78, 88, 112, 113, 118, 119
*Voice of India, The,* 70

### W

Wadia, Ava B. (*Roshani*), 116
Waithayakon, Prince Wan, 113
Ward, Mrs Humphry, 16
Washington, D.C., 12
Wavell, Lord (Viceroy), 64, 70, 73, 75, 76, 81, 86
Wellesley College, 58, 65
Wheat Loan Agreement, 85, 101, 102–3, 102 n., 103 n.
Willkie, Wendell, 60
*With No Regrets* (Krishna Hutheesing), 42, 47 n., 54, 57
Women's International League for Peace and Freedom, 53, 119, 121
Woolf, Virginia, 16
*World's Children, The* (Save the Children Fund), 48 n.
Wright, Sir Almroth, 16

### Y

Yanain, 128
*Young India,* 44

### Z

Zinken, Taya, 36

# GEORGE ALLEN & UNWIN LTD

*London: 40 Museum Street WC1*

*Auckland: 24 Wyndham Street
Bombay: 15 Graham Road, Ballard Estate, Bombay 1
Bridgetown: P.O. Box 222
Buenos Aires: Escritorio 454-459, Florida 165
Calcutta: 17 Chittaranjan Avenue, Calcutta 13
Cape Town: 68 Shortmarket Street
Hong Kong: 44 Mody Road, Kowloon
Ibadan: P.O. Box 62
Karachi: Karachi Chambers, McLeod Road
Madras: Mohan Mansions, 38c Mount Road, Madras 6
Mexico: Villalongin 32-10, Piso, Mexico 5, DF
Nairobi: P.O. Box 4536
New Delhi: 13-14 Asaf Ali Road, New Delhi 1
Ontario: 81 Curlew Drive, Don Mills
Philippines: 7 Waling-Waling Street, Roxas District, Quezon City
São Paulo: Caixa Postal 8675
Singapore: 36c Prinsep Street, Singapore 7
Sydney, NSW: Bradbury House, 55 York Street
Tokyo: 10 Kanda-Ogawamachi, 3-Chome, Chiyoda-Ku*